Love's Resurrection

By

Daniel K. Held

Higher Ground Books & Media
Springfield, Ohio.
http://highergroundbooksandmedia.com

Printed in the United States of America 2018

Love's Resurrection

By

Daniel K. Held

ENDORSEMENTS

"The battle between fear and love is one we often feel. Dan Held uses a lifetime of reflection on important theological issues to argue love can win that battle! This book is chock full of insights about God, life, and hope!"

Thomas Jay Oord, Author of The Uncontrolling Love of God, God Can't, and many more books.

"In this fascinating spiritual autobiography, through his lens as a pastor/psychotherapist, Dan Held considers his own spiritual awakenings while also exploring the spiritual awakenings in the history of the USA. He wraps both journeys around his evolving biblical understanding of salvation and the movement from fear to love. He calls us to follow Jesus on the path of love to the cross, always choosing agape love over fear. A pivotal work for our time, calling not only each of us, but our country to step beyond fear into God's embrace."

Nancy Flinchbaugh, Author of Letters from the Earth, Revelation at the Labyrinth, and Revelation in the Cave, spiritualseedlings.com

"We live in fearful times. 'Love's Resurrection,' a spiritual autobiography by Dan Held, is a beacon of hope for these troubling times. Drawing on his experiences as a psychotherapist and pastor, Dan gives a new vision to those who believe that "perfect love casts out fear. This book gives the reader many rewards and I strongly recommend it."

Rev. Michael H. Mahoney,
Retired Elder, United Methodist Church

"Dan Held grew up accepting the theology of his childhood. However, through three great awakenings, he dug deep into the truths of these beliefs in the light of his life experience. His book, Love's Resurrection: It's Power to Roll Away Fear's Heaviest Stone, is the story of his spiritual journey from fear to love and its implications for the church and our deeply-divided nation. Those who have the courage to question the "truths" they are taught ... to

challenge their fear in order to find a deeper truth ... a love that resonates with their souls ... will appreciate and be inspired by Dan's quest."

Linda A. Marshall, Author of A Long Awakening to Grace: a memoir of loss and discovery.

ACKNOWLEDGEMENTS

I would like to thank all family members, friends, parishioners, clients, colleagues, and mentors who have participated in the events described within these pages. My descriptions note a continuum of opinions I have developed over time that should be understood as only my personal opinion. Also, my memories as recorded herein are best understood as only my memories, subject to my own unique and undoubtedly fallible perspective.

DEDICATION

To my darling wife, Sue, who has shared with me these past 51 years in Holy Matrimony through times every bit as rich, poor, healthy, sick, better, and worse as we might ever have imagined when standing at our marital altar on May 27th, 1967.

CONTENTS

"When I was a young man, I wanted to change the world. I found it was difficult to change the world, so I tried to change my nation. When I found I couldn't change the nation, I began to focus on my town. I couldn't change the town and as an older man, I tried to change my family. Now, as an old man, I realize the only thing I can change is myself, and suddenly I realize that if long ago I had changed myself, I could have made an impact on my family. My family and I could have made an impact on our town. Their impact could have changed the nation and I could indeed have changed the world." -- Unknown monk, 1100 C.E.

INTRODUCTION

Fear has always had the bad habit of betraying, denying or crucifying love. Yet, in one of the most reassuring lines in all of Christian scripture (I Corinthians 13:8, NRSV), the apostle Paul has written that "*love never ends.*"

Why is that?

Why is it that fear, despite assurances to the contrary, does not trust love to "never end?" Why is fear itself afraid of love's inability to last?

Truth be told, many of us live as if it were fear that never ends. Yet, the Bible reassures us that fear can end. But that love cannot. Love endures forever.

The Gospel of Matthew reports the experience of those who were the first to discover what Christians believe was the resurrection of Jesus Christ. Along with the sight of the resurrected Christ came the sound of these words, "do not fear." The stone that was rolled away at the grave of Jesus became for the Christians of Matthew's early faith community the assurance of two new realities: perfect love really does endure forever. And fear does not.

Over the years of my own work as a psychotherapist and later a pastor, I heard several stories told by people who had what in popular vernacular is called a "near death experiences" or NDE. Per their rather consistent self-reporting about the soul leaving the body and then returning after briefly going to some proverbial "other side," two distinct experiences typically return with them. In their own words, I have heard them say things such as "it was like I was perfectly loved." And, "like I had nothing at all to ever fear, not even death itself."

Having never had my own experience of any afterlife, I still experienced something rather remarkable upon listening to others' own stories. I came through them to vicariously understand, this side of heaven, that I am also perfectly loved. And to know I now have nothing to fear, not even death itself. I am as convinced by others' powerful stories as if I'd had my own NDE.

My purpose in writing this book is to establish an important claim. It is a claim that none of us need to have an NDE in order to experience an overwhelming sense of being perfectly loved, never to fear death again. Instead, one can have this new state of mind, new peace of mind, on "this side" of eternity. One need not wait until death in this body is occurring or the soul is leaving. One's soul can deliver the same message of hopeful reassurance now. Perfect love can be discovered here on earth in a way that casts out fear, even the worst possible fear we might now image.

Love's resurrection can be experienced here on earth as it is in heaven.

Our souls can bring to mind the remarkable opposite of what we clinically label Post Traumatic Stress Disorder (PTSD). It is something I prefer to call Post Traumatic Peaceful Order (PTPO). Such a condition can trigger involuntary flashbacks concerning God's loving presence, which may cause recurrent dreams of helping other people, feelings of relaxation, hyper-compassion, and reassurance of safety. The mirror opposite of PTSD.

More than anything else, this book will introduce you to a paradigm shift involving the word, "faith." My own premise as I approach this task is that faith is a universal condition of the human mind. Faith is whatever we happen to think about the future, for lack of factual proof. There is simply no other way to face the unproven or the invisible (the future) except through the eyes of faith. Faith is what informs what the scientific mind labels one's own hypothesis. All future reality is hypothetical and unproven for the time being. It requires a mental hypothesis or faith. Such is the stuff of scientific experiments.

That said, faith is also involved in the meaning we attach to our past. To the extent we have experienced past fear, by faith we imagine a future that carries forward that same traumatic past. We use our own past to predict our own future. And we create for ourselves a self-fulfilling prophecy.

Everyone, I will claim in this book, has a fear story based on some past visible evidence projected into some otherwise invisible and hypothetical future. Universally, our human fear story is informed by some level of past traumatic experience, ranging 1-10 in intensity. There is no 0 on anyone's scale. Fear happens.

Fear hurts. Our faith in that fear then hypothesizes its way into our future's laboratory.

Fear does more than simply draw up bad future blueprints for our lives to experiment upon. Fear marginalizes people, ourselves included. Fear motivates control and retribution. It starts wars. It sickens our bodies internally and our communities and institutions externally.

Fear also separates us from God. It mirrors love's power to the extent that perfect fear casts out love, thus opposing God's will for our lives. It removes the God of love from our minds and substitutes a pseudo-god of fear. That god lives in some "out there" and "up there" position as a kind of cosmic Santa Claus with a list of our naughty deeds in one hand and a bag

of nice toys in the other. You know. For the kids on that "other list." Faith in such fear defies, not defines, the God of love who comes to save, not condemn, the whole world.

Everyone, I will contend, lives out some fear story by default, based on faith in some past memory about this untrue god of fear. This faith then projects itself upon our future in self-fulfilling terms. We participate in a vicious cycle, bringing those bad memories forward into worse fantasies which, when fulfilled, become our worst realities. It's how we sometimes go from bad to worse and how worse comes to worst. There is another name for such an endless torture: hell.

It doesn't have to be this way.

Everyone, I will also claim, can live a love story based on faith in some past but true "God is love" memory here on earth.   We don't have to wait for a NDE in heaven to serve as our game changer.

Everyone can awaken here on earth to a new faith paradigm with the power to produce PTPO. This therapeutic trauma presents a new faith in love's endurance and fear's end. It creates a paradigm of new hope and expectation. The expectation that love will come again. Love will be resurrected. And perfected. A love powerful enough.......to roll away fear's heaviest stone.

Faith in love will also act as its own self-fulfilling prophecy in our lives.

We can think of it this way: We participate in a virtuous cycle, bring those good memories forward into better fantasies which, when fulfilled, become our best realities. We really can live our best lives going forward. But it all starts with our greater faith in love. And greater doubt in fear.

It is my belief that the human mind has its own "settings" category as gifted by our creator. And that we can each change our default setting at will. We can choose to place our faith in love and our doubt in fear, not the other way around. We are gifted with the freedom to choose a reset.   The choice we make produces our own consequences (self-fulfilling prophecy).   When we choose love over fear, our decision is informed by, I believe, the very whispers of our soul. We are drawn by God's Spirit into a shared heavenly wisdom. By contrast, when we choose fear over love, our faith-decision is informed by the very shouts of our body. We are driven by our physical senses into a shared worldly ignorance.

I have come to believe that our human mind will always be conflicted by these opposing sources of information, body and soul. Love, I have come to believe, is our natural and eternal self. Our original factory default, one might say. Our God-given narrative. And that which lives on through our souls.

Fear, however, is the world's conflicting and competing default position, like a retailer that changes a factory setting to suit our own expressed preferences. The world informs our minds through our bodily senses. For some people, this means seeing or hearing a report from their preferred source of world news and feeling instant fear, triggering flashbacks in our minds having to do with past traumatic memories and future apprehension. For some people, fear becomes our dominant narrative along the way.

I know. It used to be my narrative as well.

What follows is the story of my own experience as told within the pages of my own mind. It is my own journey leading up to the re-setting of my own default. It includes my own fear story and misplaced faith before my mind's awakenings into new faith: a faith in love that refuses to wait on a near death experience. This story is about a change of mind, a change of faith, and a newly formatted default setting in line with God's factory-preferred narrative for my life on this side of "the other side." It is a story of hope. It is about love's resurrection "here and now," and about love's power to roll away fear's heaviest stone today.

CHAPTER ONE

Motorcycles and other hogs

".... for this son of mine was dead and is alive again; he was lost and is found!' And they began to celebrate." -- Luke 15:24

It was the summer of 1968. The call came in late on a Saturday evening shortly before midnight. *"Hello, Mr. Held?"* "Yes, this is Dan Held." I had just gotten to sleep, but in my new job as the on-call caseworker for Dayton's Travelers Aid Society, I was not surprised to hear the phone ringing next to our bed. And I could easily guess where the call was coming from. *"Mr. Held, this is the Medical Society answering for Travelers Aid. We need you to call a Nancy Thomas* (not her real name) *at the police station. You'll have to go through the desk sergeant on duty. He will call her to the phone. "*

I took down the number. Minutes later, after returning with a bottle of Coke from the refrigerator and my eyes opening in wider anticipation, I uttered a sincere apology to my lovely wife, Sue, as she tossed and turned toward the light now shining in her eyes. *"It's okay. I'm not asleep yet. Go ahead, Dan, and make your call, or whatever it is you have to do. Just leave the light on."*

Tomorrow was Sunday. We had no firm commitments, even though I was enrolled as a first year seminarian at Dayton's United Theological Seminary, where I would be studying to enter the United Methodist ministry and quite soon enough find Sunday mornings less negotiable. No matter what was to be on the other end of this night's phone call, Sue would support me in dealing with it even into the wee hours if necessary.

Lifting the phone, I called the Dayton Police Department's central intake number. I reached the desk sergeant on duty, who explained his referral of one Nancy Thomas, an 18-year-old white female, a stranded traveler whose identification referenced an address in Bloomington, Minnesota. Nancy, he noted, only recently arrived here in town, has no money in her possession, and wants to return home to her parents in the twin cities but does not want them contacted.   *"Would you like to talk to her?"*

"Yes, go ahead and put her on."

"Uh, hi, this is Nancy Thomas. Who is this?" "It's Dan Held.

I work for the Travelers Aid Society. I understand you've traveled here from Minnesota. Is that correct?" *"Well, yes, I think so,"* came the reply, her voice noticeably trembling with uncertainty.

"What do you mean, you think so?"

"Uh, um, well, just that I don't know where we've all been. We've been everywhere. I'm just here now and I want to get back to Minnesota. I need to leave now."

I reached for the opened bottle of Coca Cola now on the nightstand. Maybe my cobwebs were slow to clear from that sudden awakening at my bedside, but something about this girl's voice on the other end of our phone seemed quite troubling. And confusing.

"What do you mean, *'we've been everywhere?'* Who's *'we?'* Who are you traveling with?"

"Oh, no, I don't mean we right now. I'm not with anybody right now. I'm just alone trying to get back home to where my parents live near Minneapolis. The policeman here said you could help." Her trembling voice pitched even higher at the anticipation that I may or may not be trusted to help her get home. Her uncertainty was now storming into a quiver of anxiety.

"All right, Nancy, but I still need to know who you were traveling with. I don't exactly need to know where all you've been. But I do need to know why you are at the police station right now, and why you want to go home to Minnesota right now. You sound really anxious."

"Well, okay, like I mean the way I got here was with the Minneapolis Outlaws. It's a motorcycle gang. I left with my boyfriend like about two months ago or more. My parents didn't want me to leave. I haven't talked with them since. I'm afraid to call them now, but I really need somebody's help. Right away!"

"Why do you need help right away from Travelers Aid," I sluggishly responded, "and why are you at the Dayton, Ohio police station?"

"Okay, I guess I might as well tell you the story. I mean I just [seen] this police station. I was on the back of Jerry's bike. We [was] all stopped at a red light. The gang we (was) joined up with was in the lead. I just got off Jerry's bike and ran as fast as I could for this place, this police station. I figured they wouldn't come in here looking for me. But I can't stay here. I mean I gotta get out of here. I don't have any money. All I have is what I'm wearing right

now. I just have to go home. That's all."

"I see."

Well, truthfully, I didn't. But by now I was more than wide awake knowing that I, a young seminarian with a straight-laced childhood raised on a Colorado farm before attending and graduating from a small Kansas college with a newly minted liberal arts degree, was talking to some renegade motorcycle passenger expecting me to rescue her from her fright. And at the stroke of midnight, no less!

"But, I guess I don't really see why you ran from your gang," I continued. "I take it this Jerry you were riding with is your boyfriend you ran away from home with up in Minnesota. Is that right."

"Uh, I mean he was my boyfriend, and all that. I'm his old lady. At least, that's what he called me. The girls in the gang are all old ladies. I was Jerry's old lady. But when we got here to Dayton, I heard Jerry talking to some guys from the Dayton Outlaws who offered to trade them an old VW bus in exchange for his old lady, and Jerry said 'yes.' That's where we [was] going on our bikes to make that trade when we stopped at this red light outside the police station. I just freaked. I was just so scared. They were going to trade me to another gang I don't even know. For a car. And Jerry was okay with that. So I ran as fast as I could. I just have to get out of here. The police said you would help."

"Nancy, I promise I will help, but there are things we have to do first. Like call your parents. I can't help you get home tonight unless they are willing to accept you when you get there. That's the only way Travelers Aid can help you. I know it's late at night, but somehow we have to get ahold of your folks back in the twin cities."

"I know, but I'm afraid to call them," came the soft and now tearful reply. *"They hate me anyway. They'll never forgive me for running away. They'll say I did this just to hurt them, and maybe I did."*

"But will they accept you back home," I asked, "and can they learn to forgive you later if you all had some kind of, maybe, family counseling help back there?"

"I think so. Maybe. It's just that I'm so afraid to call and talk to them right now. They have no idea what all I've been through these last few months. They don't really even know about Jerry. I mean, they know he's a biker, but they don't know he belongs to the Outlaws or anything. They've just always hated him anyway, and

now I know they're going to hate me. I'm afraid to talk to them."
Her fear was now engulfed not in trembling so much as in tears.
Her soft sobbing had reached a crescendo as she spoke into the
phone.

"Would they talk to me if I called them?   Would they hate me
for calling to tell them you are okay and safe, but needing a way
home right now?"

Nancy's frightened tears turned to nervous laughter.   *"They
wouldn't hate you,"* she said, her nose sniffling as her voice softly
giggled, before finally agreeing to let me go ahead and make this
requisite phone call home for her. Moments later I placed the call,
still from our bedside phone, my wife now paying attention with her
own mix of confusion and worry. By now she, too, was wide awake
and perhaps wondering what kind of a job her husband of now 15
months had recently taken, and what this had to do with one day
becoming a Methodist preacher.

Nancy's mother answered the phone at their suburban
Bloomington residence.

By now it was nearing midnight there as well, just one time
zone removed. She, too, sounded tired to the point of being half
asleep. When told who and where I was, and where her little 18-
year-old daughter was, that she was safe but needed a way home, my
ears again were tuned to a voice of hysteria.

"Oh, my God," I heard her gasp calling out to a husband no
doubt located in the same room.

*"It's Nancy. I mean it's somebody calling about Nancy.
She's okay!"*

Turning back to her phone, *"she's where again, Ohio
someplace?"* To which I reported some basic information having to
do with her wanting to return home now but having no money for a
ticket.

More tears on the other end of the phone, only this time as a
release for pent up angst and a mother's long suffering anxiety.
"What do we need to do to get her back," she pleaded as I sat
bedside taking notes while breathing a thankful sigh of prayerful
gratitude, *"and how can we get her a plane ticket yet tonight?"*
Minutes later, our conversation resolved the plan for Mom in
Minnesota to call Northwest Airlines to arrange a pre-paid ticket on
the next flight out of Dayton. I reassured the anxious parents that
Nancy would be safe at the Dayton police station until she could be

transported to the airport for her 6:20 a.m. flight from Dayton's Cox International Airport.

Calling back to the police station, I was reconnected with the anxious teenager whose last identity, "Jerry's old lady," was nearing a peaceful end to its adolescent crisis. *"Could it be?"* she must have wondered. Could fear be nearing an end? Could this Sunday morning be the rebirth of trustworthy love? Could Nancy be, well, Nancy once again? Could *"Jerry's old lady"* be left in her past? "Could this homecoming mean a new safety, a new identity, a new freedom?" Nancy may have pondered such queries as she heard my words of reassurance that, from all her Mom had to tell me over the phone in Bloomington, her parents would be waiting for her at their Minnesota airport with open arms and loving mercy in only a few more hours. I silently prayed for God to make such possible imaginings come true for her.

In the Bible's New Testament Gospel of Luke, Jesus tells in chapter 15 a story of this Father who had two sons. The younger had left home against his Dad's wishes, only to find himself in a real mess, quite literally, some far distance from his home.

This son was dealing with other hogs. Not the kind he could ride but rather ones he was tasked with feeding. The ones whose food he'd have gladly eaten for himself to relieve his emptiness of body and soul.

It was then in these moments that son decided to make a drastic change. He felt an urgent need to go home once again to the father he had so contemptuously left in the first place. Yet he was apparently quite afraid. Afraid his Dad would hate him for leaving home so foolishly, so full of youthful rebellion. So afraid was he of even talking to his father that he had to rehearse perhaps again and again his own homecoming speech of apology. He would beg for his father's forgiveness, and accept the lowliest of jobs in his father's plantation in exchange for a place at the far end of that once familiar dinner table. He was especially hungry for his father's love, but likely, according to Jesus's story, desperately afraid at the same time.

Let's pick up that story now as written in Luke 15:20-24: *"But while he was still far off, his father saw him and was filled with compassion; he ran and put his arms around him and kissed him. Then the son said to him, 'Father, I have sinned against heaven and before you; I am no longer worthy to be called your son.' But the father said to his slaves, 'Quickly, bring out a robe—the best one—and put it on him; put a ring on his finger and sandals on his feet. And get the fatted calf and kill it, and let us eat and celebrate; for this son of mine was dead and is alive again; he was lost and is found!' And they began to celebrate."*

When Jesus told that parable of the "Prodigal Son," he may as well have meant it for all who have taken flights of fancy in this world, past, present, future. Including this 18-year-old lost sheep, Nancy Thomas, of Bloomington, Minnesota, formerly "Jerry's old lady," in the summer of 1968. And including all the rest of us who have journeyed through this world into some place of uncertainty that stirred our worst fears before begging for a place of hopeful love to finally come home to. I wonder if Jesus did not also have in mind the same message a later biblical writer would place into a letter to churches within Asia Minor. That message would contain this line: *"There is no fear in love, but perfect love casts out fear; for fear has to do with punishment, and whoever fears has not reached perfection in love"* (I John 4:18).

Prodigals everywhere and in every age need to hear that fears can end with love's new beginnings. And, hearing, all prodigals need to doubt their old faith in fear before they can choose any new faith in love.

It's our faith in fear that often stops Prodigal Sons, and runaway daughters alike, from taking that first big step into a new awakening.

We live in a world today that is traumatized by fear. It is as if our planet is not just warming by a partial degree each year but is also fearing by another degree on some imaginary 1-10 intensity scale. If last year was an 8 in terms of global fear factors, put us down for a 9 this year. We are, I believe, approaching what I would call based on Nancy's aforementioned example, a "red light opportunity." The time is approaching when we need to either get off the motorcycle and go home, or else take our chances with what the world has in mind for our future.

I say this because I've been a rider on this world's motorcycle myself. I've tried it both ways. I have my own fear story and love story to tell. I, too, have been a prodigal.

CHAPTER TWO

Identity Crisis

"There is no fear in love, but perfect love casts out fear; for fear has to do with punishment, and whoever fears has not reached perfection in love." -- I John 4:18

The summer of 1969 in America has been referenced by some as "the summer of love" due to an event most simply known as "Woodstock." The Woodstock Music & Art Fair—informally, the Woodstock Festival or simply Woodstock—was a music festival, billed as "An Aquarian Exposition: 3 Days of Peace & Music". It was held at Max Yasgur's 600-acre dairy farm in the Catskills southwest of the town of Woodstock, New York from August 15-18, 1969. It is where the word "lovefest" gained its greatest of prominence.

The summer of 1968, however, was filled with far more fear than love. As noted earlier, Nancy Thomas found herself living through a "summer of fear" after running away from her parents' home a few months prior. Love was very much in doubt, and in the distance, for her. Yet, she was not alone. Our entire nation was living through a time of great uncertainty, fear, and doubt. We were then a nation of prodigal sons and daughters, looking for love but too often in all the wrong places. It was our collective "summer of fear."

That year of 1968 started out in America with the January 5th arrest of arguably the nation's best known "baby doctor," Benjamin Spock, who along with William Sloan Coffin, the chaplain of Yale University, and a few others, was indicted and later convicted on charges of conspiracy to encourage violation of the nation's draft (Selective military Service) laws.

On January 23rd, North Korean patrol boats had captured the USS Pueblo, a US Navy intelligence gathering vessel and its 83-man crew on charges of violating the communist country's twelve-mile territorial limit. This crisis would dog the US foreign policy team for 11 months, with the crew of the Pueblo finally gaining freedom in late December.

On January 31st, at 12:30 on a Wednesday morning, the North Vietnamese had launched the Tet offensive at Nha Trang. Nearly

70,000 North Vietnamese troops took part in this broad action, taking the battle from the jungles to the cities. At 2:45 that same morning the US embassy in Saigon was invaded and held until 9:15a.m. The Tet offensive would continue for months on end, inflicting heavy casualties against our American and South Vietnamese troops.

On February 1st, during police actions following the first day of the Tet offensive, General Nguyen Ngoc Loan, a South Vietnamese security official was captured on film firing a fatal bullet into the head of a terrified Viet Cong prisoner. The Pulitzer Prize-winning photograph taken by Eddie Adams would become yet another rallying point for anti-war protestors.4

On February 7th, international reporters had arrived at the embattled city of Ben Tre in South Vietnam. Peter Arnett, then of the Associated Press, wrote a dispatch quoting an unnamed US major as saying, *"It became necessary to destroy the town to save it."*

On February 18th, the US State Department had announced the highest US casualty toll of the Vietnam War. The previous week saw 543 Americans killed in action, and 2547 wounded. Televised images of America's best and brightest being shipped home in body bags became a part of our evening news during a time when most American families still ate an evening meal together with these nightly telecasts often in the visible background.

On April 4th, Martin Luther King Jr. had spent the day at the Lorraine Motel in Memphis working and meeting with local leaders on plans for his Poor People's March on Washington to take place later that month. At 6pm, as he greeted friends just below in the parking lot, King was shot with one round from a 30.06 rifle. He was declared dead just an hour later at St. Joseph's hospital.

Sen. Robert Kennedy, hearing of King's murder just before he was to give a speech in Indianapolis, IN, delivered a powerful extemporaneous eulogy in which he pled with the audience *"to tame the savageness of man and make gentle the life of this world."* Yet, the King assassination would go on to spark street riots in the cities of Baltimore, Boston, Chicago, Detroit, Kansas City, Newark, Washington, D.C., and elsewhere. Across the country 46 deaths were blamed on the riots.

On April 11th, United States Secretary of Defense Clark Clifford called 24,500 military reserves to action for 2 year commitments, and announced a new troop ceiling of 539,500

American soldiers in Vietnam. The total number of Americans *"in country"* would peak at some 541,000 in August of that year.

On April 23rd, a rally to protest Columbia University's participation in the Institute for Defense Analysis resulted in an illegal student occupation of five buildings - Hamilton, Low, Fairweather and Mathematics halls, and the Architecture building. It ended seven days later when police stormed the buildings and violently removed the students and their supporters at the Columbia administration's request.

On the night of June 4th, upon achieving victory in the California and South Dakota Presidential Primary elections, Sen. Robert Kennedy addressed a large crowd of supporters at the Ambassador Hotel in Los Angeles. As he left the stage, at 12:13 a.m. of June 5th, Kennedy, too, was shot to death by an assassin's bullet.

On July 7th, Abbie Hoffman's "The Yippies are Going to Chicago" was published in a paper called *The Realist.* The yippie movement, formed by Hoffman, Jerry Rubin and Paul Krassner, all committed activists and demonstrators, was characterized by public displays of disorder ranging from disrupting the trading floor of the New York Stock Exchange to the destruction of the Clocks at Grand Central Terminal, the main commuter station for workers in New York City. The Yippie's would become the center of action six weeks later at the Chicago Democratic National Convention, hosting a "Festival of Life" in contrast to what they termed the convention's "Festival of Death."

These and so many other events in 1968 were all stirred together and baked into a year of heightened uncertainty and fear for Americans everywhere, not only for Nancy Thomas and her Minnesota family.

On a very personal front, my own life was going through a time of fearful uncertainty as well. What I am about to tell you about my own critical state of mind during that time period may make you cringe. There's a chance you will read on and find my experience relatable. There may be a greater chance you will read past this point to find it contemptable. Or some of both. I can only account for my own mind's whereabouts that year and no one else's.

During the summer of 1968, I had enrolled at United Theological Seminary in Dayton, Ohio while also taking a part-time job with a local social service agency, Travelers Aid Society. I would soon begin classes in this new and unfamiliar setting. I was anxious about my own future, because the call to ministry I was beginning to discern was not a pulpit and worship ministry after all. It was taking on more the appearance of a counseling ministry in which I would reach out to those suffering the greatest amounts of anxiety and depression and relational dysfunction. I was awakened at night by things other than calls from the Travelers Aid answering service. Questions in my own mind about why I was on the verge of entering seminary to become a minister. Questions I felt restless to get answered. As a staunch opponent of our nation's war in Vietnam, was seminary for me only a means by which I would dodge the draft into military service? This so-called Vietnam *"conflict"* was, I believed by the time of my graduation from Sterling (Kansas) College in May, 1968, an ethically unjust war. It was both undeclared and illegal. Not to mention unethical by any academic standards of just war theory. I felt deeply uncertain that summer on the verge of my seminary coursework, like a horse who had just wandered into a stable full of cows. And that uncertainty often awakened me more at night, even more than did those calls from our Travelers Aid answering service.

I was tormented, both night and day, by what I then perceived as a blatant hypocrisy on the part of my own nation. Our independence from England's colonialism was purchased at the cost of so much bloodshed, yet we were now flirting with a colonialist role of our own in the sovereign nation of Vietnam, whose own Ho Chi Minh was acting out precisely the same role and function as did our own General George Washington. No wonder General Ho, as he was called, had become such a hero in his homeland. No wonder Americans were now replacing the colonial Frenchmen as the hated people of Vietnam. I imagined another European nation following the British exit at the hands of our revolutionary army, invading our own newly claimed homeland and seeking to defeat our General Washington themselves. This would have made no sense! And so our military invasion of Vietnam to defeat General Ho ourselves made no sense to me. It was the cruelest form of hypocrisy I could imagine.

Adding to my own torment was the fact I had friends and family members serving in the military, some even in Vietnam. They disagreed vehemently with my take on the war back then, and probably still do. I affirmed their right to disagree with me then and still do even now. And I validate their own fears of communism every bit as much as my own fear of American hypocrisy.

Then there was America's Civil Rights movement. My nights of uncertainty in the summer of 1968 filled me with fear as I began my studies at what amounted to an all-white seminary except for one black Associate Professor and a handful or two of dark skinned international students. I sensed a racial colonialism here in 1960's America no less unjust toward our people of color, including the native Americans, than the British colonialism had been for our nation's anti-colonial forefathers. And I sensed our nation's Protestant Churches of 1968, so segregated along racial and cultural lines, were no less complicit in supporting our colonial efforts than were the Anglican Churches supporting the British King George III of 1776. Like Pogo Possum of comic strip fame would later declare, I had met the enemy and he was us. This was another cruel form of hypocrisy I was troubled by.

No, Nancy Thomas was not alone in her fear. Even I felt like running away at times from the very choice I had made to become a parish pastor in the Christian Church of that time in our nation's history. Many of my fellow seminary students seemed far less troubled about all that was going on in our world and nation that I was. I found myself, perhaps wrongly, judging them as being servants of a civil religion that gave God's blessing away to those of our fellow Americans who were colonizing other people both at home and abroad. Some were seeking to become military chaplains, likely to serve in Vietnam. This in spite of our deep American roots in anti-colonial rebellion and revolution. "Whatever happened to the Golden Rule?" I wondered silently within my insomnia. I harshly judged even my own peers in 1968 by questioning their own judgment in support of our status quo.

For me this summer of fear in 1968 was like a dubious motorcycle ride of my own into who knows what or why. I had some questions circulating through my mind that were demanding answers. The gang I belonged to was my own Christian church denomination. Would my church appoint me to serve as an itinerant minister in support of American civil religion in some "other" place? Or would I somehow escape into the alternative story of God's use for me in some counseling role perhaps helping families such as Nancy's through their own prodigal story? Could I be hearing and understanding toward others' heaviest of fears, and still find my own voice as a messenger of God's love?   Could I honestly say my faith in God's love was every bit as real as I knew my own fears were?

The answer for me in the summer of fear marking 1968 was, simply, "I don't know."

Fearing my draft induction in support of an unjust war, I would go on to remain in seminary until, at the red light of President Nixon's 1970 declaration of a 90-day Selective Service Moratorium to begin that next January, I jumped off and ran into full-time social service agency work. I shifted my academic studies over to The Ohio State University for a Master of Social Work degree more in tune with my discerned call from God into a counseling ministry.

Nancy Thomas was a metaphor for my own prodigal story. And not only mine, but perhaps for America at large in that summer of fear. The summer of 1968.

Yet Nancy's flight into the unknown as she prepared for her own prodigal homecoming may have in some way symbolized everyone's life at some stage or another. That summer of '68 represents any stage in time where our worst human fears seem to eclipse our view of love's presence or its perfection and power to live on when all else dies. Nancy's fear story was every prodigal child's story.   Faith in fear seemed greater than faith in love.   Until a crisis came along that forced some new wide-eyed awakening.

As I approached my 22nd birthday in 1968, I underwent an identity crisis having not only to do with my career path routed through a theological seminary, but around the broader issue for me of national patriotism.   That was the year in which a bumper sticker was introduced and prominently displayed on thousands of cars and trucks reading, AMERICA: LOVE IT OR LEAVE IT.   I could do neither of these.   In my mind there was a fear that my own nation was wrong in its foreign policy.   I feared America was blind to the strong comparisons between Vietnam's revolutionary General Ho Chi Minh and our own revolutionary General George Washington. Had we become "traitor" to our own cause and somehow betrayed our own nation's revolution by taking up American arms against this populist leader of another nation's anti-colonial struggle?   One who had already fought its own revolutionary war against France.   And won!

What followed Ho Chi Minh's unexpected victory in Vietnam's own war of independence in the 1950's was indeed that country's use of an eastern Communistic Socialist model instead of the western Democratic Capitalist model of economic politics. But so what? Why should they be endeared to any model of western colonial economics as was followed by their French capitalist enemies? By the time of my seminary admission in 1968, I was uncertain of my own political or economic preferences. After all, western capitalism was also at the very heart of the African slave trade upon which our nation's own economy had long depended. Who could blame the victims of capitalist colonialism for seeking out an alternative economic system?

Another vehicular bumper sticker affixed throughout our nation that year was: MY COUNTRY RIGHT OR WRONG! I had been raised to believe that America was always right precisely because of our anti-colonial revolution against imperial Great Britain, and later on our anti-slavery victory in our civil war against the confederate states. Portraits of George Washington and Abraham Lincoln hung from the walls of my elementary school classrooms growing up. I had come to love my own country as a patriot. I stood proudly to observe the 4th of July fireworks, to sing about our home of the brave, and to pledge my allegiance to our one nation, under God, indivisible, with liberty and justice for all. Bring on the Stars and Stripes forever! America was always right. And I was a proud citizen!

As the great grandson of a Union Army soldier from a northern Illinois infantry, I was proud of our nation's Civil War victory, defeating the pro-colonial model of slavery. We were an anti-colonial nation that fought for liberty and equality, and I was proud of our revolution. I loved my country and had grown up believing America would always get it right! I personally lauded our past war victories against both England's colonial control over Americans and the Confederacy's colonial control over negro slaves. Let freedom ring! Hurrah for the red, white, and blue! With liberty and justice for all!

My collegiate studies at Sterling College had included a course in International Relations where Vietnam was portrayed as being a north and south Civil War only one decade after winning their Revolutionary War against colonial France. By contrast, America's Civil War between north and south followed our revolution by some eight decades. Astonishingly, Vietnam's Civil War was hastened by our nation's secondary (some think primary) role in stopping their reunification election of 1954 in which their own nation's General, Ho Chi Minh, was nearly certain to become their first President along the lines of our own General George Washington? Now, only 14 years later, we were fighting to help South Vietnam essentially defy, and secede from Vietnam's own sovereign union. I imagined, say, some powerful foreign nation supporting America's southern confederacy against our Union Army. Or eight decades earlier interfering in our election of General Washington. What if another nation linked to our own southern slave-dependent economy had invaded our nation to "free" our own South for their obvious economic advantage? Our own Civil War might have then had a horribly different outcome if such a foreign nation interfered with our sovereignty. So I believed our nation was horribly wrong in Vietnam supporting the South's secession there for the sake of their version of "free" trade with our western capitalist economy.

This truly called into deep question my own beliefs about free-trade capitalism that goes in search of cheaper labor for the sake of higher profits. I agreed with private ownership for individuals but not really for corporations. In the mold of Thomas Jefferson, I treasured free family enterprise but scorned the idea of free corporate enterprise. I had grown up on a farm in Colorado started by my great grandfather, who as an American Civil War veteran had benefited from America's Homestead Act of 1862. Our national government had provided land as capital so he could move to Colorado and start his own farming and ranching business, and raise a family. This was a privilege afforded such white European American families as mine. I was thereby a direct recipient of the Caucasian American Dream. My own college education was paid for by my parents' participation in that dream.

I supported our nation's free and private enterprise system because I believed in my own family. Yet, this same family had also raised me in a Christian Church that taught me the difference between supporting and worshipping. I had learned to believe only God was always right, and that all other powers, including that of human economic systems, were corruptible and unworthy of idol worship. Where my family left off, my college instructors had inspired my critical thinking in response to right and wrong, good and evil. The extent to which American capitalism so loved money and idolized "profitability" that it used the cheapest possibly labor, i.e., slavery, to achieve significantly higher profits, meant in my own mind that God was always right but America sometimes did get it wrong. Yes, freedom to own other people as private property, for instance, was a part of the culture throughout the Bible. But no, I couldn't find any verses where God, or Jesus in His name, said such a culture was good or alright. Rather, God went to a great deal of trouble to free the Hebrew slaves, and Jesus spoke of his own mission to *"free the oppressed"* (Luke 4:18) and also taught, *"Therefore, whatever you want men to do to you, do also to them, for this is the Law and the Prophets"* (Matthew 7:12). I found such a teaching by the Jesus I was calling "Lord" to be rather compelling, along with a saying I'd learned as a child in school then attributed to our President Abraham Lincoln: *"As I would not be a slave, so I would not be a master. This expresses my idea of democracy."*

My childhood identity as a patriotic American and a devoted Christian called into professional ministry was somehow at stake in the summer of 1968 as a soon to be 22-year-old. Some would call it an "identity crisis." It was a time of fearful uncertainty in my life. Was I still a proud American and a dedicated Christian? If drafted into our military, would I become a soldier of misfortune for the American military's pro-colonial mission? If entering the church's pastoral ministry, would I be the unwelcomed voice for change trying to challenge some status quo "My Country Right or Wrong" parish? What would become of me? What would tomorrow bring if I stayed in seminary? If I left seminary?

CHAPTER THREE

Saturdays and beyond

"Being attached to the problems of yesterday
or the insecurities of tomorrow will destroy
your today." --Steve Maraboli

An identity crisis may mean different things to different
people. For me, it means being full of doubt where once I had been
full of faith. Picture a limp balloon on the floor that once hugged
the ceiling. It is still identified as a balloon. But not a very faithful
one.

The year of 1968 had seemingly sucked the air out of my
"faith" balloon. Or at least sucked the certainty out of my mind.
By year's end, I wasn't certain what to believe or trust in. My faith
in love seemed in doubt. My faith in fear was starting to take shape.
I was becoming afraid for the world. For my own nation. My own
church. My own life and future. And this "fear story" out of which
I was living was dragging on slowly. 1968. 1969. Even into 1970.

My first two years of seminary were, for me, something like I
imagine the Saturday in between Good Friday's crucifixion and
Easter Sunday's resurrection was for the original disciples of Jesus.
I was filled with feelings of doubt and uncertainty. Looking back,
this specific time for me was my worst identity crisis ever. Yet
looking all the way back to the biblical Gospel stories, I wonder if
the time between the crucifixion and resurrection was not the worst
identity crisis ever for those original disciples. Far worse than even
my own crisis.

Their Lord was gone. He was dead. Crucified. Buried in a
tomb that, according to the synoptic Gospels of Matthew, Mark, and
Luke, consisted of a hole cut into a wall of stone and then covered
with a giant rock that was rolled across the tomb's entry.

Yes, this was their Saturday. They were filled with doubt and
uncertainty. Their identity was in question beyond all imagining, or
all preparing in advance. They were no longer certain of who they
were, whose they were, or what would become of them. They were
still Jews and today was their Sabbath, but could they feel free to
enter the synagogue? Would they be welcomed? Or even safe?
They knew only bad news. They were eye witnesses to the

crucifixion of Jesus, if only from a distance. What they did not know as yet was Easter Sunday's really good news. So they could only live with Saturday's uncertainties. And hang out, the Bible suggests, behind locked doors nearly immobilized by their own fear.

Truth be told, don't we all go through times of fearful uncertainty in our lives? Days in between yesterday's death and tomorrow's resurrection. Days when we lose our sense of safety, security and even our identity. Days, or sometimes years, when we are in transition. Unsure of who or whose we even are. Uncertain of what tomorrow will bring. These are our own Saturdays.

We all have them.

And for a while, we all close ourselves off in some way that lets us feel a bit safer and more secure. We all have days of withdrawal and retrenchment. And doors to hide behind.

There is a sense, I realize now in looking back to those years of 1968-1970, in which I withdrew to my work as an on-call caseworker with Traveler's Aid for a safe place in which I could answer God's call to ministry. This without having to test any parish's reaction to my revolutionary message of Jesus Christ. I liked getting those phone calls and going to work trying to help those who were in some way stranded travelers new to our community. I could practice what I considered to be Christian hospitality much in the vein of Christ's parable of the sheep and the goats: *"for I was hungry and you gave me food, I was thirsty and you gave me something to drink, I was a stranger and you welcomed me, I was naked and you gave me clothing, I was sick and you took care of me, I was in prison and you visited me"* (Matthew 25:35-36). And maybe even be an agent of change for some prodigal sons and daughters along these lines: *"So he set off and went to his father. But while he was still far off, his father saw him and was filled with compassion; he ran and put his arms around him and kissed him"* (Luke 15:20).

Nancy Thomas found herself booked on a flight home to uncertainty. I can only imagine what it was like for her after we spoke our good byes and she was left with only my word that her parents in Minnesota would welcome her home from Ohio, where her prodigal rebellion had produced this night of desperation. Her summer of 1968 was not ending overnight. Her Saturday night may or may not have awakened to a Sunday of perfect love in the Thomas household. I wondered if she, aboard her plane out of

Dayton, may have rehearsed her own prodigal's arrival-speech to her awaiting parents at the Minneapolis-St. Paul International Airport. She was running back home as fast as she could. But what was she running into? Would Sunday be better, or worse, than Saturday's brush with the Outlaw gang's planned car- swap now behind her? Would her fate be to sit at the far end of some servant table from now on? Might that have been her worst fear upon returning home that Sunday?

The 20th chapter of John in the Bible's New Testament describes a dramatic account of Sunday morning fear in the lives of Jesus's followers. It begins with a report from Mary Magdalene to two of his closest disciples, John and Peter. Her fear was that someone had stolen Jesus's body from his tomb, for when she went early that morning to visit his grave, it was opened. The stone was rolled away. The tomb was empty. A robbery had been committed, or so she thought. Her message of fear was shared with John and Peter, who thus took off running to the tomb. Upon their arrival, they also found the stone rolled away. John feared even going inside until after Peter had first checked things out. John, though probably writing his own first person account of that Sunday morning, made no reference of their return to Mary Magdalene, nor any attempts on their part to calm or reassure her. Nor did John and Peter seek out the other disciples right away. Instead, John reports, they both went to their respective homes as if to avoid further notice.

They hid. Again.

Later that evening, John reports that the disciples of Jesus except for Judas, now perhaps dead, and another named Thomas, had returned to their place of communal hiding. There was more safety in numbers. Doors were again locked. Sunday had come, but not all was immediately well. Saturday's fears were still in evidence. And the disciples of Jesus, other than Mary Magdalene herself, were primarily concerned with their own safety and survival. It would take a miracle to pry them from their hiding place.

In walked the miracle. It was the resurrected Jesus. Now in front of them, bolted doors still in place, Jesus spoke as if to calm them down, *"Peace be with you."* They heard the words, but even then John gives no evidence they were ready to relax. Jesus then appealed to their sense of sight, showing them his bodily scars of Friday's crucifixion.

Yet again Jesus said, *"Peace be with you."*

Finally, through the combination of miraculous sight and sound, they were able to actually relax and rejoice. Jesus then breathed on them as only a living person could do. Saturday's awful uncertainties and natural fears were finally driven away.

But none of this reportedly happened overnight.

For that last disciple, Thomas, John's 20th chapter continues to relate just how slow Saturday's fears and uncertainties were to leave. Hearing it from the other disciples was still not enough. *"But Thomas, one of the twelve, was not with them when Jesus came. So the other disciples told him, 'We have seen the Lord.' But he said to them, 'Unless I see the mark of the nails in his hands, and put my finger in the mark of the nails and my hand in his side, I will not believe.'"* (John 20:24-25) Only later on would Thomas have such an opportunity to face up to his severe uncertainties. The resurrection would only then be able to roll away his heaviest fear. *"A week later his disciples were again in the house, and Thomas was with them. Although the doors were shut, Jesus came and stood among them and said, 'Peace be with you.' Then he said to Thomas, 'Put your finger here and see my hands. Reach out your hand and put it in my side. Do not doubt but believe.' Thomas answered him, 'My Lord and my God!'"* (John 20:26-28)

Jesus overcame death by his own resurrection well ahead of his overcoming doubt by his own disciples. Therein lies an important lesson for us all. Faith in love's resurrection here on earth and this side of heaven requires a series of encounters with the risen Christ. There's no such thing, I would contend, as a single come-to-Jesus meeting on earth that settles our faith once and for all. Faith in fear is tested over time. But so is our faith in love.

We all need more than a single Easter morning encounter. More than a simple one-time encounter to transform our faith from known fear to unknown love. Or from known death to unknown resurrection. We all need Saturdays and beyond.

And that is true not only for us.

It was also true for the disciples of Jesus. Yet, they would all go on to eventually lead lives based on a faith in love's resurrection, fearless to the extent that all remaining disciples at the time of that first Easter except John would go on to die a violent martyr's death. So sure were they of the resurrection that their faith in eternal love over temporal fear led these ten men into martyrdom with Christ. Accounting here for only two disciples, Peter would die years later from his own crucifixion upon a cross turned upside down. While Thomas, by Coptic Christian accounts, was killed by decapitation after refusing to renounce his faith in Christ's resurrection.

Doubts really can end in faith.

Fear stories can end in love stories. Not in a seamless, uninterrupted way without uncertainty. But despite uncertainty. As the 1960's came to a close, I was still living out of my faith in fear. And, consequently, living out of my doubts when it came to love.

What would come next, I wondered.

CHAPTER FOUR

Easter awakenings

"Don't believe everything you think."
--Byron Katie

Much is made of the word "*awakening*" in Christian history. Typically, the word denotes a specific period of religious revival and social transition. Invariably what American historians have labeled a "religious awakening" has followed a period of social uncertainty and doubt not unlike what I would call, borrowing from the original disciples of Jesus, "Saturday fear" with its own heightened insecurities. A period of common fears and distant loves. Yesterday's certainty of pain and tomorrow's uncertainty of relief. Arguably, our own nation has known at least three such periods that fall under the classification of "Great Awakenings." Here, then, is a background description of America's religious "*awakenings*." Note that none happened overnight. None involved a seamless transition. Such awakenings never are that simple or sudden. "Saturday fears" don't go away overnight for us. Nor did they for the original disciples of Jesus that brought some doubts with them from that day before his resurrection.

Between April and December 1721, thousands of Bostonians contracted smallpox, and hundreds died from it. October was the worst month, with 411 deaths. Smallpox caused more than three–quarters of all the deaths in Boston that year. Smallpox was a very old disease, with evidence for its presence going back centuries. In Europe and the United States, bouts of smallpox were considered to be almost inevitable, and the disease was greatly feared. In some populations, the impact was especially severe: After being introduced by 16th-century Europeans, smallpox is said to have killed most of the indigenous (Indian) population of North America.

Cotton Mather did not originate the idea of small pox inoculation in the Massachusetts colony in 1721. Rather, he borrowed the idea from his negro servant named Oollnesimus. Owing to its successful practice in Africa, Mather became convinced this was the best defense against this horrid epidemic now ravaging his community. Convincing others would, however, require all of his skills of persuasion, and then some. Those in his own parish condemned this idea, arguing that epidemic diseases afflicted the people for a divine reason and any attempt to prevent them would certainly oppose God's will.   Others argued that inoculation, with its roots in Africa, was a heathen practice not suitable for Christians. Most Boston physicians, as well as the general public, argued with equal passion against inoculation on the grounds that it could spread the disease rather than prevent it; that it could cause a fatal case of smallpox in the inoculated subject by making that very subject susceptible to other diseases. Unfazed by this public criticism, Mather went ahead with his servant's old African practice and injected his own son with a small amount of the smallpox virus.

Strange, then, that Cotton Mather would help light the torch for what, commencing in this same decade, would come to be called America's 1st Great Awakening. He would do so with a long line of frightened countrymen and women tiptoeing behind him. Yet, follow him they did because his work was casting doubt upon fear itself and a new faith in God's love for the sick. As Mather was himself newly awakened and transformed, he chose to live out of God's preferred love story for his life, thus abandoning the fear story (Salem witch trials) that had made him famous. As his own faith and doubt switched sides, others in his large sphere of influence were better prepared to follow suit.

Mather was the essential catalyst for this work of Great Awakening carried forward by those such as Rev. Theodore Frelinghuysen, a Dutch reformed Pietist, who began to see revival signs of conversions following his ministry in New Jersey. That revival spread to the Scottish-Irish Presbyterians under the ministry of Gilbert Tennant, whose father, William, founded the famous 'Log College', which later became Princeton University. The prior epidemic of fear and doubt became a new epidemic of faith spreading soon to the Baptists of Pennsylvania and Virginia, the Methodists of Georgia under the banner of George Whitefield, all related to the extraordinary awakening located in Northampton, Massachusetts, under the ministry of Jonathan Edwards and lasting into the following decade.

It was this same Jonathan Edwards who shared this description of results from that Great Awakening in his 1737 treatise entitled, *A Faithful Narrative of the Surprising Work of God in the Conversion of Many Hundred Souls in Northampton:* *"There is a very great variety, as to the degree of fear and trouble that persons are exercised with, before they attain any comfortable evidences of pardon and acceptance with God. The awful apprehensions persons have had of their misery, have for the most part been increasing, the nearer they have approached to deliverance; though they often pass through many changes and alterations in the frame and circumstances of their minds. Sometimes they think themselves wholly senseless, and fear that the Spirit of God has left them, and that they are given up to judicial hardness; yet they appear very deeply exercised about that fear, and are in great earnest to obtain convictions again.* "1

Perhaps such a context as Edwards noted is not all that far removed from the one Jesus described as belonging to the prodigal son: *"When he had spent everything, a severe famine took place throughout that country, and he began to be in need. So he went and hired himself out to one of the citizens of that country, who sent him to his fields to feed the pigs. He would gladly have filled himself with the pods that the pigs were eating; and no one gave him anything"* (Luke 15:14-16).

Edwards then writes what may be the most telling of all descriptions for this Great Awakening, using these terms, *"Persons are sometimes brought to the borders of despair, and it looks as black as midnight to them a little before the day dawns in their souls."* 2

That was our 1st Great Awakening in American religious history, dating back to the 1730s. It was grounded in a period of great fear and great uncertainty associated with the 1720s smallpox epidemic in New England.

So now consider this background for the 2nd Great Awakening.

If the 1st Awakening had pulled America into a time of greater enlightenment, daring and discovery, the 2nd Awakening began on a much different note.

A mix of many American historians have suggested that the Revolution brought by the colonists against Great Britain brought with it a host of great social challenges. As it all turned out, protesting was much easier than actual governing. Organizing for what we were against turned out much easier than organizing for what we were for. Socially, economically and politically, the American Revolution may have been both the child of our 1st Great

Awakening and the parent of our 2nd awakening.

The inevitable vacuum in governance resulting from our freedom from British rule brought about another full-fledged Saturday, of sorts, for our American society. No longer cohered around our common British enemy, we began as a people to turn on each other with vitriol and violence. Shay's Rebellion, along with ethnic and class-based urban disturbances took their toll. Conflicts around slavery erupted in forceful argument, never to be resolved. The late 1790's gave way to more of the same social fragmentation in the new 19th century, opening the door ever so broadly for a fear this time not of disease but of violence.

Religious society, as administered by the Protestant churches, led the way in organizing the new nation around their own models and methods. Though not quite a theocracy, the Church held considerable influence upon American government during this rather infantile period of the latter's development. Into the vacuum created by having to actually govern now that the work of protest and revolution was accomplished, religious society began to set the new norms for organization. With non-violence. Reformist Presbyterians and Anglican Methodists set forth some very important new norms of governance.

If Jonathon Edwards was the eventual face of America's first awakening, then likely Charles Finney was the face of the second. Finney, though Presbyterian in background, stressed a Christian holiness that would begin at the church or camp altar but extend into social living through the work in abolition of slavery and increasing equality of women. American universities were inspired by an emphasis on social holiness. Colleges like Yale University began training clergy for our churches and new colleges were founded like Oberlin in Ohio, where Charles Finney agreed to serve as the school's second president on the condition it would admit black persons and guarantee "free speech" to all its students. There at Oberlin College, Finney stressed a religious agenda for the reform of American society even acting through government and the law. Indeed, the struggles and conflicts and uncertainties of our nation's earliest decades had given way to a new 19th century in which new churches were organized in nearly every outpost west of New York City.

That was considered to be our 2nd Great Awakening dating back to our post-colonial period of the 1790s. Its context was not a fear of epidemic disease so much as epidemic freedom. By this I mean that in place of our responsibility to the British colonial monarchy came a kind of social irresponsibility and a new tyranny of open conflict that came with it. New norms of social responsibility were needed to fill the vacuum. And new religious and educational organizations would offer a stabilizing effect upon the new nation.

For a while.

This newly organized United States was still a work in progress, to put it most generously. Just as Sunday's new love follows Saturday's great fears, so another Saturday rolls around yet again on the next week's calendar. The Protestant Church had grown by leaps and bounds in the 50 years from 1790-1840 thanks to the 2nd awakening, but that awakening's greatest blessings, its new social organizations, would soon become the nation's greatest curse.

Its curse came in the form of such newly formed Church groups as the Millerites, who had gotten the word out far and wide that Christ would return to earth between March 21, 1843 and March 21, 1844. When this did not happen, William Miller, the leader, reset the date at October 22, 1844, and again those who had trusted his prediction were disappointed and infuriated. So widespread was the clamor that even the general churches who had nothing to do with the Millerite delusion were mocked. As happened prior to other religious awakenings, the people simply did not know what or whom to believe anymore.

Such social uncertainty produced, as it often does, a period of economic volatility. By October, 1857, America's banks were failing, which destroyed consumer confidence to the degree that future investment narrowed, railroads went into bankruptcy, and financial chaos arose at all levels. A civil war seemed unavoidable to many because of the slavery question. America tottered on the brink of disaster. This time our fear story was not about disease or violence, but more about poverty.

The 3rd Great Awakening in America began ostensibly in New York City as a prayer meeting in the year 1857. Within six months 10,000 people were gathering daily for prayer in numerous places throughout New York. In a short time, the New York Times reported that the nationally known pastor, Dr. Henry Ward Beecher, was leading 3,000 people in devotions at Burton's Theater. Once while he was reading Scripture, Beecher was interrupted by singing from an overflow prayer meeting crowd in an adjoining barroom! By his own uncanny improvisation, or many would say the Holy Spirit's movement within him, Beecher then led his theater attendees in prayers of thanksgiving that such an interruption from the barroom could even happen. Other major cities also developed prayer meetings. The form of worship was always the same: any person might pray, give a testimony or an exhortation, or lead in singing as he or she "felt led."

Although pastors such as Beecher often attended and lent their enthusiastic support, laypeople provided the leadership. Little planning was done for the meetings, the chief rules were that a meeting should begin and end punctually, and that no one should speak or pray for very long. In Chicago, the Metropolitan Theater was filled every day with 2,000 people. In Louisville, Kentucky, several thousand crowded each morning into the Masonic Temple, and overflow meetings were held around the city. In Cleveland, the attendance was about 2,000 each day, and in St. Louis all the churches were filled for months on end.

That was considered to be our 3rd Great Awakening covering roughly the 50 years from 1857 - 1907.

My point in mentioning all of this is by now quite plain. Great Awakenings grow out of times of great change, great uncertainty and great fear. Such fear takes on an organic life of its own, struggling to survive, grow, and gain control by any means possible. The dominant public discourse feeds a national narrative or fear story aimed at acquiring control. When such control proves to be an illusion, then a vacuum appears into which steps a new faith in love's influence that proves far more real or true. This involves a spiritual conversion of sorts, otherwise referenced to be a religious awakening. Fearful control breeds vast uncertainty, whereas loving influence brings about new certainty.

Taking that into account, I am one who now contends for the existence of a 4th Great Awakening in America. I believe it was initiated on the streets of Hollywood, California in the year 1969. That's right. The year after one of America's most turbulent of so-called Saturdays of fear and uncertainty.

What happened on the streets of Hollywood was the appearance in October of 1969 of a new newspaper called the Hollywood Free Paper. Its humble origins centered around an experience Duane Pederson had as a young minister seeking

relevance on the gritty boulevards of Hollywood, California.   What
Pederson noticed within his own street parish was an abundance of
publications offering opportunity to score drugs, sex, and whatever
else might awaken some higher consciousness within the people of
his community. He observed that every street intersection was lined
with newspaper racks offering what he considered free but lurid
tabloids of underground activity.   Passersby would often grab not
one but several papers promoting a range of possible "heights" of
new personal discovery.

It was then, in October of 1969, that Duane Peterson launched
his own publication. It would identify his mailing address as a local
PO Box 1949. Within days, his mailbox began filling up with
inquiries. Who was this Jesus the paper was writing about? How
could readers learn more? Was there a place to meet for discussion?
When could they expect more answers? Calling his publication the
Hollywood Free Paper, he would place first tens, then hundreds, then
thousands of papers in the neighborhood newsstands.   New issues
would be posted on the first and third Tuesdays of each month.
This went on for seven years. At its peak, half a million copies were
taken from newspaper stands each month.   And a "Jesus movement"
would be born in Hollywood that morphed into new faith
communities gathering for discussion and Bible study under names
such as Vineyard and Calvary Chapel.

When viewed sequentially, these four religious Awakenings in
America have been a series of "come to Jesus meetings,"
homecomings for prodigals, and opportunities to find out more than
we ever knew before about who God really is. There is a common
denominator among these awakenings in which participants
experience a new doubt in their former fear that God hated them and
was destined to punish them eternally. With that new doubt has
come a new faith that God loves them and has a preferred love story
for their lives far truer than the old fear story in which they
previously suffered.

What they further reveal to me is that even larger societies and
nations can transition in between narratives, reaching critical points
in their fear story that finally parks them at some fork-in-the-road
decision point. The wrong choice can create our communal fear's
heaviest of stones. The right choice can create our communal love
story's own resurrection.

Notes:

1. A Faithful Narrative of the Surprising Work of God, Jonathon Edwards; Baker Book House, Grand Rapids, 1979 paperback edition, ISBN-10: 1537518208

2. Ibid.

CHAPTER FIVE

Lights in the distance

"Everything you've ever wanted is on the other side of fear."
-- George Addair

All of the historical Great Awakenings have at their heart a fear story that moves in search of a love story that offers people more actual truth. Each awakening at any level, from micro to macro, from personal to communal, is a work in progress. A trajectory of positive influence comes into play. A newer and truer narrative takes shape and then takes place. The transition from fear story to a new story always moves toward a loving direction, but multiple transitions and awakenings are apparently required. There is no one-time fix. Truest stories require a series of truer stories along the journey. Truth itself is a continuum. And I would say this is true for our nations and our personal lives alike.

So permit me to share more about my own personal life as I began my own series of Great Awakenings, all containing some share of fear and trembling along the journey.

I can account presently for what amounts to my own three Great Awakenings. Each one began with some measure of heightened fear in search of some higher love that would more truly define my existence. Each existential crisis in my own life has required some new "leap of faith" forward.

Whatever the source, there is a fable told about twins in the womb having their first ever argument. One of these fetal twins believes there is life after birth in the arms of an unseen but still very real Mom. The other does not believe in Mom. Mom is unseen and therefore unproven. What's more, there cannot be life after birth. They have no such evidence. This womb is all there is. And so the argument goes. As in any contest between a believer and a non-believer, neither is able to convince the other to adopt a different faith.

Over on "this side" of such a fable, we know with certainty there is life after birth and that the dark womb is left behind and the prior uncertainty about the "other side" is like a bright light that awakens. Both twins, once in conflict, are now in agreement. Both share in their own great awakening oblivious to any prior dispute.

End of argument. But only after the "other side" becomes "this side." Where fear is concerned, love is always on the "other side" before its light can awaken us on "this side." Takes a while to see the light. Sometimes a long while.

Before commenting on my own birth into this world back in August of 1946, and that pull toward my own "new" world's first awakening, I'd like to reflect just a bit on a familiar verse from the Christian New Testament found in the Gospel of John 3:16. *"For God so loved the world that he sent his only begotten son, that whoever believes in him will not perish but have everlasting life."* The context, of course, was a conversation Jesus is having with a man named Nicodemus, to whom Jesus earlier says in 3:3, *"Very truly I tell you, no one can see the kingdom of God unless they are born again."* Both of these verses, I believe, are foundational for understanding the so-called Christian Gospel. Yet, not in the way we traditionally understand them.

The full context for these two verses involves the story of Nicodemus, a man whose final encounter with Jesus would come after his crucifixion, when he helped in preparing Jesus's body for burial (John 19:39). John 3 is about his first encounter with Jesus. Then Nicodemus, a Jewish Pharisee, came to Jesus in the dark of night when no one of his peers might notice.

Darkness, and this is a key to understanding John's Gospel concerning Jesus, becomes the central metaphor by which his readers are to understand not only Nicodemus himself, but especially these familiar verses of 3:3 and 3:16. Darkness is the very context in which we all live as human beings. Nicodemus is more than just a religious leader of his times. He is, I suspect John would have us believe, an allegory for every human in every place and time. We are all in the dark when it first comes to faith in God's love that follows our own fear. Like Nicodemus, our faith is first in our fear of God and not in God's love of us. Such a transition of faith requires a new awakening or new birth. Until then, we remain in the dark womb of our current faith, which is in our fear of God's punishment, doubting God's universal love for all.

The foundational message Jesus had for Nicodemus concerning salvation is that God's love for the world requires doubting the darkness of our fears in order to be born into the light of God's love. Concerning the doubt Nicodemus had about such a new birth, Jesus says, *"The light has come into the world, and people loved darkness rather than the light"* (John 3:19).

Said differently, many of us would rather die than change. We would rather perish than have everlasting life. We are all like Nicodemus when it comes to doubting God's bright light of universal love. We would, in terms of our own belief systems, prefer staying blind in the darkness of faith in our own fear of God's punishing damnation of this world.

And so we all, like Nicodemus, really need to be born again even though Jesus defines this in his new birth narrative as letting go of our old faith in the womb of darkness. And instead following the light of God's heavenly Kingdom that so loves the world. Spiritual rebirth carries the same risk and benefit as does physical birth for the infant entering the strange light of new uncertainty. John 3:16 is but an important mile-marker along that journey beyond the womb in which we will otherwise perish if our birth fails.

Being born again, as Jesus makes clear in John 3, is all about seeing the light of God's world-wide love after first believing in the darkness of God's anger and punitive damnation.

Such is the preamble to my own fear story in search of my truer love story. I was Nicodemus upon my first coming to Jesus.

So I was born into a world of strange and powerful light, my first experience with any "other side" becoming a true "this side" of life. My earthly parents, Clarence and Mildred Held, were wonderful. As were my three living grandparents and my older sister, Ramona. My Christian parents had great dreams for me upon my birth in the small town of Sterling, Colorado during that new baby-booming summer of 1946. Both Dad and Mom were third generation German-American farmers. I would be presented by my parents for Christian baptism at our small rural church when I was but an infant. I would be raised in the church and all would be done to assure that my life would fulfill my parents' dream for me to be a dedicated Christian farmer and father to my own son(s).

Well, not so fast there. Baptism, it turns out, is a place our own dreams go to die and God's truer dreams are resurrected.

The sacrament of Christian Baptism is traditionally centered around our repentance of sin that then gets washed away even as we are re-born by the Holy Spirit into righteous living. It is an outward sign of God's inward grace in our lives. It is our initiation into the Church of Jesus Christ. Depending on which scriptural verses are taken to be more foundational, Christians differ as to age requirements for this ritual or sacrament. So when I was baptized as an infant, my parents presented or some may say sponsored me in line with the Philippian convert named Lydia and, in another case, the Philippian jailer, both from Acts 16. Their entire families were baptized with them based on their own parental faith and commitment. By implication, these parental believers had special privilege over their family members in securing God's grace for them as well. So Mom and Dad, as Christian believers, spoke their vows for me renouncing the powers of evil and sin within us all, while re-affirming alongside our welcoming congregation their own saving faith in Jesus Christ.

In the truest sense of the term, baptism was for me a darkness to light passage with everlasting significance.

By history, the church has viewed baptism as our identification with Christ in both his crucifixion and his resurrection. Biblically, we read from the Apostle Paul such words as, *"For you were buried with Christ when you were baptized. And with him you were raised to new life because you trusted the mighty power of God, who raised Christ from the dead"* -- Colossians 2:12.

In most Christian traditions, baptism would seem to carry forth some transition from fear to love, or from crucifixion to resurrection. Perhaps this would take the form of our past sinful uncertainty being exchanged for the certainty of God's grace in forgiving those sins. For some Christians, infant baptism conveys a certainty about a child's identification with Christ from the beginning of life in this body. For other Christians, believer baptism conveys a certainty of identification with Christ as a matter of personal decision. Likewise, for some Christians, a tiny handful of water conveys certainty of this new identity in Christ, while for others a full immersion below the water's surface is needed to convey that same certainty. Regardless, the common denominator among Christians is that baptism removes some faith in our worst fears and replaces it with a faith in our greatest hope, our identification with the risen Christ.

In the tradition of my own Protestant Church as a child, my family lived under the Wesleyan tradition that believed the Christian faith happened in stages moving forward from infant baptism, which in its own rite celebrated God's prevenient grace in our lives. I was then raised in the church with my parents' own vow of confirmation and our congregation's own litany of affirmation. This involved their covenant to nurture me in the making of my own decision to accept salvation through Christ as I came of age. By this I mean that baptism launched me on my way to the next stage of faith we in the Wesleyan Christian tradition call God's justifying grace.

There is within Wesleyan Christianity and its Methodist traditions a kind of dance that occurs between what I'm calling faith in fear and faith in love. Baptism removes our faith in fear and replaces it with our faith in love. Yet, sin continues and fear of sinning persists. And because it does there is another new faith that comes to replace our old doubts. Round and round we go on life's dance floor. These back and forth dance steps symbolize also an exchange between our own humanity and God's divinity (beginning with Christ's own baptism) that strikes a rhythmic pattern of sin and grace, fear and love, or darkness and light when applying John's Gospel.

At the risk of throwing around too many metaphors here, I'd like to suggest that in my own case this back and forth was what brought about my first Great Awakening during my teenage years. If baptism was my first step onto faith's dance floor, it truly did set the tone for a back and forth journey leading to my first genuine conversion experience at summer church camp in the Colorado Rockies' Temple Hills Campground.

It was nightfall at the campground. The outdoor chapel area was our assigned gathering point for what amounted to an old fashioned service of Christian evangelism. All campers were assembled. A bonfire was lit in the distance some 30 feet to the front of our chapel benches. Between that fire pit and ourselves stood the conspicuous presence of an old rugged cross representing the place Christ died for our sins. And while I can't now recall any particular mention of such, the implicit meaning behind these two frontal visuals was that Christ's cross alone would come between ourselves and the fires of hell into which we would otherwise fall given the downward slope of our chapel along the hillside.

The chapel preacher that evening raised the questions at least by implication. Were we in any way uncertain of where our souls would depart upon death, whether heaven with Jesus or perhaps into the eternal flames of hell? Were we in any way afraid that hell may await us on account of our sins? If so, we could become certain that very moment by first raising a hand and then, as the chorus of "*Kumbaya, My Lord*" softly echoed in the voices around us, walking forward to stand beneath that old rugged cross and professing our faith in Jesus Christ for our eternal salvation from the nearby flames of hell.

Which is exactly what I did.

Along with several others standing next to me in front of those chapel benches, the preacher at that night's campfire service had us repeat a ritual prayer of personal confession and invitation for Jesus Christ to save "me" from "my" sins that otherwise would send "me" into one hell of an eternal bonfire when "I" died.

In looking back, I can see two important dynamics at work in that teenage experience of conversion. The first, of course, was the faith I had in what I now call my dominant fear story. The only way to gain control within this story, the only way to fight off of my fearful emotions, was to perform this ritual of going forward to whisper beneath my own breath, eyes tightly closed, the magical prayer of personal confession.

That was one dynamic at work. Had I have been the only one going forward that night from the campers in my midst, it would have been the only dynamic.

However, a second and even greater dynamic bears reflection as I now look back. Not only was I not the only one going forward that night, but I was not even the first. Several others among my camping peers stepped in front of me to go forward, boys and girls alike. They were about to gain a certainty I was yet to claim. I wanted what they, too, were wanting. This most important dynamic at work is what some would call communal desire. None of us transition from a fear story to a love story alone. There's always a community of influence at hand. More about this in my final chapters.

The late Rene Girard is a Christian anthropologist whose study of human cultures revealed a universal trait of communal influence he calls "*mimetic desire*," as in imitating the desires of our own community and culture. We shun our universal human pain of uncertainty by first coveting and then grabbing ahold of whatever seems to satisfy others' desires for certainty. Upon experiencing our own fears and uncertainties, we imitate those who seem less afraid and more certain. We all experience this communal influence along our life journeys as we are awakened beyond the womb. Advancing in our social development, we sometimes call our continued communal influence by the name of "peer pressure."

Wanting what others have is a communal desire that follows

each of us through adolescence and even beyond. One such desire I would later experience growing up was that of adult vocation as necessary if I were to ever enter my adult love story. Marriage and children one day would hitch their wagon to a vocation of some sort affording an actual livelihood. So by the time I graduated from high school, I had applied and been accepted to a college I had not even visited except by catalog, recruiting letters, and the testimony of a couple different high school friends. By June of 1964, only two months from starting into this rather fearful unknown in my life having to do with a hoped for adult love story, I found myself at another turning point. Call it the last leg of my first Great Awakening.

It happened at another church related event. This time in the beautiful environs of Colorado's Red Rocks Amphitheater. I was with our Youth Fellowship group from church as we attended a Christian concert featuring, among others, a group named Thurlow Spur and the Spurlows. It was sponsored by the Denver Youth for Christ organization. And amidst this idyllic setting under the stars, I found myself getting up from where we were sitting as a group and wondering around the amphitheater a while until reaching, at one point, the upper ground level overlooking all the seats below and yet still hearing the great music reverberating off the tall red rocks reaching from stage below to parking lot above. There, amidst the interplay of music, message, and the starry majesty above, I received a stirring within that I considered to be God's call for me to enter Christian vocational ministry as my career path.

This was for me a very different experience of awakening than I had at the campfire a few years earlier. This time no human voice was questioning me or challenging to make any kind of decision. None of my peers were around me. I was standing alone. There was no one else to imitate, no one else's certainty to desire. No peer pressure in the direction of any such career path. I was being "called apart" to serve the God of my own certainty. No faith in fear was involved.

This was no "come to Jesus" meeting on the part of any church calling me forward. This was a "go forth from Jesus" meeting on the part of God's Spirit sending me outward. Only my confirmed faith in love was involved.

That experience marked a moment of reflection about the college life and later adult vocation that would assuredly await me.

And my heart was once again strangely warmed, as John Wesley would say, while standing that evening beneath the starlit sky of the Rocky Mountain foothills, the lights of Denver off in the lower foreground, and accepting my call to enter fulltime Christian ministry. Total faith in God's preferred love story for my life was now mine! I now grasped precisely where college would take me. And this would complete my own first Great Awakening.

So far so good. But it was only the beginning. I was then only 17 years old. My own dance of fear and love, doubt and faith, sin and grace was only getting underway.

CHAPTER SIX

Wilderness journeys

"Wilderness is not a luxury but a necessity of the human spirit."
-    Edward Abbey

If my first Great Awakening took 18 years to develop, the second would take place over the course of the next 38 years.

As mentioned in chapter two, my arrival in Dayton, Ohio in the summer of 1968 after graduating from Sterling College brought with it much doubt and uncertainty about both my nation and my church. Together these separately great institutions seemed complicit in privileging the rights of white Euro-Americans above those whose skin color or ethnic culture was different.   I was beginning to put away some of my childish thinking and to grasp more of what God's love story for this world might potentially look like. Yet, I found no new institutions to immediately devote myself to either trusting or serving. I began doubting whether this love story was real after all.

It's noteworthy to consider that it was an educated Christian apostle named Paul who associated childish thinking with his own past, only to realize that in adulthood we still looked through the glass dimly. Which is another way of saying that the more we learn in life, the more certain we become of life's many uncertainties. Part of increasing in our human certainty is knowing for sure how little we know for sure. Sometimes our biggest step of faith begins with a series of small steps into doubt. Faith in the new wine of Jesus requires first doubting the efficacy of our old wineskins. By the time I reached seminary, I was only one step into that process.

Seminary for me was something of a reinforcement of my prior years at Sterling in learning to think critically about the world around me, including the church but also the very creeds upon which the church seemed anchored. Though attending classes full-time, I would also work as the after-hours, on-call caseworker for the Dayton Traveler's Aid Society, as well as in full-time casework during summer breaks from seminary.

Much of the work demanded of a caseworker within such social service agencies as ours at Traveler's Aid involved social advocacy.   In other words, I would be tasked with advocating for social solutions to personal problems that had overcome the clientele we were serving. I was something of a paid Good Samaritan binding the multiple wounds to body, mind, and soul of strangers in our streets and highways. The aforementioned client I referenced by pseudonym as Nancy Thomas exemplifies how it is that our personal choices as humans can produce unintended and sometimes overwhelming consequences for ourselves. My work with Traveler's Aid advocated for the stranded and the stranger as if serving Jesus himself in that process.

In the classroom, much of what I remember about my early seminary experience was that I came to appreciate the Kingdom of God as being central to the biblical message and the Christian Gospel. Earthly kingdoms posed as idols in our world and drew us away from the actual work of God in the world, which involved advocacy for individuals whose personal problems required social solutions. In a very theoretical sense, seminary exposed me to an understanding of the Kingdom of God as being the ultimate social solution for this world of troubled individuals. Jesus brought this solution to earth as God's advocate for all of troubled humanity, but he did so one troubled person at a time. Think caseworker! However, my old wineskins of faith had not been sufficiently emptied, and much of the new wine of Jesus was wasted at that time in my life. New theories and theologies came out tasting rather bitter when poured into those old paradigms of faith left over from my teenage years. Said differently, my faith in the fear of God's hell-bent wrath remained something of a barrier to any new faith in God's universal love for all humankind. My fear of human nature itself remained strong as well. I was living on the border between my own love story and my own fear story. I was in the throes of an identity crisis with a faith in fear gaining ground in my life.

Looking back at this point in my story or history, I see where this represented the end of my first Great Awakening that had occurred in my teen years. I was a few short years later in the earliest stages of a re-awakening. This journey would take far more than the 18 years from my baptism to call into pastoral ministry. It would gather considerable steam over a period of another 3 decades plus. I was then walking, not jogging, along the journey I'm now calling my 2nd Great Awakening.

For reasons of uncertainty about the institutional Church's role in advancing God's Kingdom where it was needed most, I deserted the seminary classrooms pretty much in midstream. I dropped out of school amid my second year, taking a full-time caseworker position at Traveler's Aid. I began plans to enroll elsewhere for a Master of Social Work degree that would position me for service in a counseling ministry I felt God was instead calling me to enter. This would enable me to provide high quality clinical care for those who could not otherwise afford to purchase such help. For this reason, I enrolled at the Ohio State University while under the employ of Dayton's Family Service Association, the umbrella agency locally for Traveler's Aid Society.

If United Theological Seminary, during the year and a half worth of classes I had attended, afforded me a greater sense of uncertainty, then Ohio State for those next two years would seem to answer back with what seemed to be a more reasonable certainty. A career in clinical Social Work could be my way of helping troubled individuals, marriages, and families find adequate social solutions for their most personal of problems. Where God's Kingdom was concerned, I doubted its relevance in today's world and rather quickly replaced it in my own mind with what, back in the day, was called the "human potential movement."

As with many clinicians looking back to the years of training and early practice, I shudder to think of the many mistakes I made whether diagnosing or treating my counseling clients. By the time I was fitted with my graduate stole as a newly minted MSW in Columbus, I was struck by how uncertain I really was about my own abilities. I had mastered the science of knowing I could cure no person of any disease at all, and that at best I could try taking some difficulties in life my clients would present and note a few patterns that might have impeded their somewhat easier lives. At least some of the time. For even if I caught the right patterns, motivating others to work past them and try a different line of thinking or acting was often beyond my grasp.

The remainder of the 1970s were, for me, a time of great trial and error professionally. I was reasonably well liked by my clients, colleagues, and superiors in the field, but as I sat for my Academy of Certified Social Workers (ACSW) exam in 1978 after my requisite practice years, I realized that everything I knew in way of theories carried no practical guarantees in the real world. Passing a lengthy exam proved nothing beyond my theoretical comprehensions.

The 1980's would bring about opportunities for more

specialized training through the University of Cincinnati's department of Psychiatry within their College of Medicine. In particular, the Family Therapy Training Center within this department would provide me with more focused workshop training and laboratory experience. I say laboratory meaning only that my clinical work with families there at that Center would be observed by colleagues behind a one-way mirror, videotaped, critiqued, and modified under the direct supervision of Dr. Marion Linblad Goldberg. After two years of this training, I did feel a great deal more comfortable in working with troubled marriage and family relationships as presented in my Dayton, Fairborn, and Xenia offices of Family Service Association. My level of certainty bumped up at least a few notches during these years.

The 1990s found me changing jobs to work with a somewhat more troubled clientele found within Dayton's Good Samaritan Counseling Centers. Commensurate with these more difficult clinical cases, I trained a great deal more within the areas of Cognitive Behavioral Therapy and in Narrative Therapy, the latter being a post-modern approach to family therapy mostly imported from Australia and New Zealand.

Meanwhile, the clinic where I worked contributed an overflow of opportunities to meet with an amazing assortment of clients in search of help to resolve often deep-rooted problems of living. One client, among hundreds, I remember seeing was a man named Thomas Nance (not his real name) who came to me with a provisional diagnosis of Bipolar disorder. At least this is what Thomas was told by a previous mental health provider. He was taking no medication at this time, but was actively drinking alcohol as needed to sedate himself and coax a bit of sleep out of each otherwise sleepless night. He was being divorced by his wife (his presenting problem) who expressed privately to me her fear that he would eventually murder her in her own sleep. Thomas privately conceded that he had a nasty temper but blamed this on his wife's leaving him, alongside the stress of his last of many job terminations. He considered himself misunderstood and underappreciated, and by habit was prone to long verbal rants that had alienated even his own parents and one sibling. He confided that since his time in the Army infantry during Vietnam, he had suffered from some combination of flashbacks, nightmares, and phobias. He admitted it didn't take much to "set off" his nerves.

Thomas believed his own pursuit of happiness would require getting his wife and kids back and gaining some better control over his temper. As he saw it, the former would in itself take care of the latter. Having his family back together would calm his nerves and angry temper if I could only help salvage his marriage for him. His wife, perhaps understandably, refused to participate in that fantasy.

My own unspoken goal for Thomas was to hopefully help him avoid prison or the cemetery, whichever came first. He denied having suicidal or homicidal ideas or intentions. He abhorred the idea of a hospital bed. So the best I could do was bargain with him for a trial of out-patient medication from our clinic psychiatrist to replace his alcohol use if he still wanted to calm his nerves. Thanks to public funding, our clinic and its 24-hour crisis line managed to provide enough daily and nightly accountability to last through his transition from alcohol to a more controlled sedative and mood stabilizer as an out-patient. For many weeks on end I met with him individually and in group therapy. As was typical for persons with a bi-polar depressive disorder, Thomas would consider some amount of mania to be essential in fighting off his most painful of post-traumatic anxieties and major depressive symptoms. Like some persons I'd seen before, Thomas also had an obsessive-compulsive component to his mania, which turned out to work in his favor in that he never missed a scheduled appointment with me nor was even a half minute late. He was meticulous in his own grooming and attire, yet equally demanding and impatient with others he derisively judged as slobs. Once entirely sober from alcohol, he became rigorously obsessed with maintaining that sobriety. Slowly he would come to terms with his own marital termination, which came before his acceptance of the estrangement he had with his now late adolescent children.

One thing Thomas Nance and I were both learning in the course of our time together in counseling was that uncertainty was certain. Yet there was progress to be made in just naming and understanding these old uncertainties. Every week or two would bring about some new uncertainties. At least they would not be the same ones now left behind in the past. No more Viet Cong and NVRA. Now only the coalition of enemy forces named PTSD, Bipolar Depression, and Alcoholism were after him. They now seemed far less lethal than before. If viewed as a prodigal son in relation to his own treatment goals, Thomas had at last left the pig farm behind with the hope of maybe gaining a place on the far end of the servants' table one day.

For Thomas that day did come, though it was much different from anything either of us had ever expected. Having spent many months of therapy utilizing Thomas's old soldier metaphors for fighting against the enemies of disease, learning how they would seek to trick or trap him, knowing how they worked together and when and where to expect their attack, figuring out his best defense, something very different now entered the picture. It carried its own treatment plan that, frankly, I had every doubt in mind could have possibly worked for the good. It was a religious experience he would have at a Pentecostal church service a neighbor of his had invited him to attend. To open his next counseling session with me, he could barely wait to tell me, "I've been born again." It was as if he had finally arrived back in his Father's arms.

As with most clinicians of my ilk, hearing such words from a client battling bi-polar disorder at any level triggered my immediate suspicion of medical non-compliance or hyper manic relapse. But in asking him to tell me what happened, Thomas explained that three nights ago he accepted an invitation from his neighbor to attend some local "revival" service. He described it as being the most liberating and cleansing experience of his whole life. His sins were "forgiven." He was "saved." He was a "new man." These were all descriptors he used for his new sense of being as "a Christian."

Karl Menninger, the famed psychiatrist, once said that if he could convince his hospitalized psychiatric patients that their sins were forgiven, 75 percent of them could be discharged the next day! But I was never really able to buy that myself. Especially when my faith in fear was dominating my faith in love at such points.

So I listened to Thomas that day with a great deal of suspicion. His speech was appropriately measured, not in any way pressured. His thoughts were organized clearly and concisely. No ideas of reference. No looseness of association. No flight of ideas. Nothing to suggest any manic break from reality at all. No mood lability. Just a soft-spoken presentation with full range of affect, and a warmer smile than I'd ever seen before on Thomas's face.

Hmmm. I wasn't sure quite what to think.

My reply came about rather deliberately. "Well, that's great, Thomas. I'm a Christian myself. But how do you think that's going to affect your war effort when you have to deal with these other enemies you've been dealing with? Dealing with sin and guilt is one thing as you say, but dealing with those other problems like Bipolar and PTSD is something very different." I was uncertain of what to otherwise ask him, and just as uncertain of how to answer his next response. He told me he was now unsure he would need to even continue that other fight. Unsure he really had any of those earlier disorders or even needed to continue taking any of these medications he was on for his own mood stability. He supposed he would stay on them for a while but would ask the doc if he could come off of them gradually over time. While he "might" like to continue coming in to see me for counseling, he "most definitely" planned on returning to church and continuing living by this new religious awakening he had experienced. For him this had been the most awesome spectacle to behold in this world. It was as if peace had broken out everywhere and he was now free to drop his weapons of war and actually love his enemy.

Thomas Nance would say all the right words as he continued on in his session, explaining what it meant for him to be reborn in this way. I was the one who alone was uncertain. Thomas expressed a certainty, and even a mood stability, I had never seen before.

Given this occasion, my own self-talk as a clinician was to explain this as what old school therapists called "a flight into health." As if by habit, I found myself inoculating Thomas with a warning that, now borrowing from his own new experience, Satan would try especially hard in these coming days and weeks to use Bipolar Disorder to bring him back down again by sending him up into the clouds and then dropping him. This did seem to resonate with him a bit.

For the next year, Thomas and I did continue to meet for counseling, albeit with less frequency. Uncertain as I was at first about his newfound faith in Jesus for salvation, I felt relieved to know he would stay on his medication each day and stay away from any alcohol relapse. He would also continue to express normal regrets and even resentments but not to any extreme. His temper would still flare at times, but at a slower pace. He would continue going to church on a regular basis.

To his great credit, Thomas got a job that actually fit his personality traits and nocturnal insomnia to a tee. He would stock shelves in a local supermarket at night. His fellow church member was a store manager there, and it proved a good fit. Thomas would not only stock shelves, but take some delight in turning each product "label out" as only someone with obsessive-compulsive traits can enjoy doing. Besides, the night job excused the fact he had always done his best sleeping during the day.

More than most, clients with bipolar depression produce uncertainty on a day to day basis. Sometimes an hour to hour basis. The only certainty truly is uncertainty, and the best one ever achieves is a kind of stable instability. Avoiding too much stimulation or stress becomes a general theme in such cases. But waiting for the other shoe to drop always feels familiar when dealing with persons like Thomas Nance. Or at least that had been my own anecdotal impression to that point.

Yet, this is really true in everyone's experience to some degree, I've come to believe. We all have the capacity for a religious Great Awakening only to drop from some new level of faith in our lives into some even newer level of doubt. Only to need yet a better Great Awakening to come.

I can say this especially because I would soon come to need my own better Great Awakening to come. Better than my original back in the early 1960's. My need was triggered by a phone call one morning.

It was early in October of 1999 when a call came from Sue's family living out of state. This single phone conversation would change our lives forever and would challenge even the best of our own coping abilities as individuals even in the most committed of marriages.

First, a bit of background. The family I married into had five children of which Sue was the 3rd, with an older sister, an older brother, and two younger brothers. All of these siblings lived hundreds of miles from us in all different directions but were in close and regular contact with each other.

So that October morning, we answered our phone in Ohio only to hear the mind-numbing news that her youngest brother had taken a knife and killed all three of his kids before attempting to kill his wife and himself. His wife was in the local community hospital while he was in their local County Jail.

By way of further background, this youngest of Sue's siblings had been out of work for most of the past year but did have a Ph.D. in pharmacology from one of the country's leading medical schools, had a reasonably strong career, and was at last report seeking to start his own niche business within his expert field of forensic pharmacology. He had no prior arrests and, like all men in this family, had been a high-achiever from his childhood on through his professional positions of high responsibility. What is more, he was a professing Christian very active in his own local church.

I told you this call would change our lives forever and would challenge even the best of our own coping abilities!

The long shadow of uncertainty this news then cast upon our lives as a family could not even be estimated. It was vastly bigger than my own confused mind could wrap itself around. In the hours, days, weeks and months to follow I found myself living in the darkest mood of my entire life. That particular Fall day in 1999 remains for me a movie in slow motion as I recall nearly every event that followed that phone call. By late afternoon, Sue and I were stepping off the jet-way at a distant airport to meet her sister and mother, gathering up our luggage for an indeterminate stay there, and meeting another brother-in-law as his mini-van pulled up to the "Arrivals" curb outside the terminal.

Our first stop was at the hospital an hour north of the airport where our dear young sister-in-law lay in her hospital bed, bandaged about as only a stabbing victim can be. Still in shock but fully alert, she was able to tell us much of what had transpired in their home the night before. The event occurred on the 10th anniversary of my father-in-law's death, and had by all present appearances been a planned, premeditated murder-suicide. After this violent act, this badly injured young lady miraculously survived enough to escape to their next door neighbor's when her husband took off in the family car. He was later that same night apprehended by police while bleeding from his own self-inflicted cuts to his own throat. After a trip to the closest hospital trauma center, he was transported to the County Jail and placed on suicide watch.

For those who have dealt with acts of such violence in your own family, perhaps you will relate in knowing that uncertainty becomes one's only certainty after such an event. No matter how many answers one receives, there are always more questions remaining unanswered. And, for me, one of those questions was wondering why I didn't see this coming at all. Other than to exchange a few emails in recent months, I'd had no communication with this young family since their relocation from an eastern seaboard state to their current residence out west. They had stopped overnight with us back in June while driving across country by car and U-Haul truck.   They were tired of traveling that long day, but the kids were their usual happy selves and quite playful with our family pets during their visit. The oldest son was 7. His younger brother was nearly 5. The baby sister was 2. That night we had feasted on spaghetti with Cincinnati chili, an area favorite, and all seemed to eat well, sleep well, and communicate as if no serious problems might be in the works. Yet, in retrospect, I feared there was something I had missed in the process. In fact, I was living out of my worst ever fear story. Fear's heaviest stone was covering up my faith in love. It was as if my own love story had just died with these three children. I began doubting my own ability to accurately assess and help people in need.

Perhaps others have felt this same way after a violent tragedy within their own family.

On our first full day with family, we paid our first visit to Sue's little brother at the jail where he was held. We took short turns using the phone across from our respective, glass- divided cubicle. He was attired in an orange paper gown with bandages about his own neck. He had little to say other than "I wish I could fly away from this whole deal right now," which I thought was a bit odd. However, to me everything in the world seemed odd that day and nothing at all was normal anywhere I looked. Life itself was more surreal than anything I had ever experienced before.

It's interesting to now recall in hindsight that 1999 had been a year when I felt my first itch to actually retire one day from my work as a therapist. It was something I'd never even considered previously. I would turn 53 that year and after 25 years in counseling work, I had a sense in which I would sort of coast to some finish line in the next 10 years and then retire to an easier life for a change. However, the church Sue and I attended was Ohio's Ginghamsburg United Methodist, where Rev. Mike Slaughter was then the lead pastor. One Sunday morning in worship, his sermon had words for me that seemed to blow a hole in my own retirement aspirations.   I have no idea what his text or title of message was in retrospect; only that the take-away for me that day was that God didn't want me to ever retire. No, God wanted me to retrain or retool or get ready for a new career in ministry beyond the counseling clinic. God wanted me to recommit to a life of pastoral service without thought of retirement.

For me this meant thoughts of actually going back to seminary and exploring the possibility of somehow finishing my abandoned seminary degree. Perhaps I would figure out even some role for myself in full-time church ministry somewhere ahead. Well, maybe.

Alongside that experience of uncertainty then simmering beneath my surface, this was the year I had also taken on a new workplace role involving more administration of mental health programming, something I quite frankly was not cut out for and found more than a bit frustrating and stressful.

So even before that tragic event, I was not claiming my life to be all that I wanted it to be. I was ripe for a change. Almost any change but what actually did transpire on that particular October night.

Nonetheless, there I was with family out of state for nearly a week using some paid bereavement leave and a couple days of borrowed vacation. Trying to wrap my head around this crisis of child-murders within my own dear family of in-laws. And having to face some events I found more difficult than anything else I'd ever had to deal with, even among clients at work who had themselves been suicidal or even homicidal. This was far more surreal. I felt more uncertain than ever, and more afraid of the unknowns to come.

How I handled this fear was that I became more controlling over my immediate environment. If others were indecisive, I stepped in to make the decision. If others were in some way hesitant, I took charge. This was rather unusual, to say the least.

I was the in-law from Ohio. Married into this family some 33 years prior, but still enough of an outsider that I should not have been so quick to take charge. Yet, I found myself acting out the role of a family therapist and, for that matter, a family pastor who would gather folks into a prayer circle. I would initiate the hugs. I would take charge in approaching the three little white caskets at the funeral home prior to the community visitation there. And when comforting other mourners among the immediate family, I was first to offer words of reassurance. Many of these words, I now know in hindsight, were entirely inappropriate. Yet, my tendency in the face of my own fearful uncertainty was to act out my own control needs. I would take charge, even if it meant placing my foot in my own mouth. I would say "I know" even when I clearly did not know. All so I could feel a sense of control in the face of my own dreadful fears.

After viewing these beautiful children lying in repose at the funeral home, one of the most unforgettably tragic and mournfully sad times of my entire life, we stood around to comfort family until friends from the neighborhood and even church began making their own entrances. Then, in my own controlling way, I pulled Sue aside and said we were borrowing a car to run down to the jail for a visit with her little brother once again.

No doubt Sue was torn when it came to staying with her family or going along with my decision, but she supported me without argument and we left together for the 20-minute drive down to the county jail. What happened next can only be described as my internal argument between all the fear and all the love bottled up within me in that hour.

I took my Bible in with us for the jail visit as permitted by authorities there. Upon his arrival at the visitation cubicle where the attached phone receivers were separated by thick glass, I told him that I had something I needed him to hear that wasn't from the family or me or anyone else. It was from God. Then I proceeded to read these words from Romans 8: *"Therefore, there is now no condemnation for those who are in Christ Jesus, because through Christ Jesus the law of the Spirit who gives life has set you free from the law of sin and death. For what the law was powerless to do because it was weakened by the flesh, God did by sending his own Son in the likeness of sinful flesh to be a sin offering"* -- (Romans 8:1-3).

I wasn't at all sure I even believed these words in my own heart or even mind. All I knew was I wanted to control something about which I was most uncertain. And afraid of.

Then I followed my reading with these words found later on in that same chapter of Romans: *"Who then is the one who condemns? No one. Christ Jesus who died—more than that, who was raised to life—is at the right hand of God and is also interceding for us. Who shall separate us from the love of Christ? Shall trouble or hardship or persecution or famine or nakedness or danger or sword? As it is written: 'For your sake we face death all day long; we are considered as sheep to be slaughtered.' No, in all these things we are more than conquerors through him who loved us. For I am convinced that neither death nor life, neither angels nor demons, neither the present nor the future, nor any powers,* ^{neither} *height nor depth, nor anything else in all creation, will be able to separate us from the love of God that is in Christ Jesus our Lord" -- (RO 8:33-39).*

Why was I working so hard to control whether this murderous young man felt condemned by God or not? Why did I want him to be so certain he was not going to be condemned by God? Honest truth: I was so afraid this brother-in-law, whom I had genuinely liked prior to all this, was going to be condemned by God for the murder of these dear, innocent children. I wanted so badly to condemn him myself. And I was uncertain if I would ever be able to forgive him. Indeed, I was struggling inside just to control my own rage after visiting the coffins of his three murdered children. Therapist or not, Christian or not, I was a human being first. And my first human instinct was to fear for his own future and to control against my own anger at him. In my own controlling way, I was desperately afraid and longing for love wherever I could possibly find it. So I turned to Romans 8, doubts and all.

There's a sense in which all the uncertainties I had ever faced in life up to this point were now dwarfed by this new uncertainty involving my own emotions. I felt afraid as never before within my own body and my own mind. And I sought control over everyone in my presence as if to then reassure myself as well.

Next day at the funeral for our nephews and niece, I found myself reacting with fear and rage at the area television media camped out in their satellite vans and adjacent sidewalks. Their photographers were shooting live footage of the coffins being carried out of the church. I urged all mourners then waiting outside to circle the hearse and the family limo and provide a blockade from the camera to protect the privacy of our young sister-in-law and her immediate family members following the coffins. Let them have pictures of our backs but not their faces, or coffins. As I turned to see one station's cameramen climbing a tree to gain a shot over the top of this blockade, I found myself offering an obscene finger gesture at him while still standing outside the church for this sacred ceremony. My fear story had just done what most do in due time: turned to rage in search of control. In all my new doubts about love, it was if I was now playing a God who sent others to hell!

Prior to our return to Ohio two days later, Sue and I joined with our family members, our sister-in-law and her family members, in a conference room of the local county prosecutor and that office's

Victim Witness Advocate. We were informed how the laws of that state would proceed through enforcement, noting that our family member was being arraigned on capital murder charges, that the prosecution would be seeking the death penalty, and that the State itself would be appointing a team of attorneys from the state capital who represented all capital murder defendants. This team would be in contact with us as needed in the weeks and months, perhaps even years, to come. Meanwhile, the Victim Witness program itself would provide services to his wife and her family for as long as they would deem necessary. This was of real comfort and reassurance to us.

We were further informed that our family member would be exposed to a prison culture at every level that provided more condemnation of child victimizers than we might ever have imagined. We were inoculated against the strong possibility that he would be violently assaulted himself while awaiting execution or even trial itself. While ambivalent emotionally about our own love and hate relationship with this little brother at that point, we felt a great sense of fear about future news we might one day receive about him. In that meeting with prosecutors, I found myself again speaking out of fear to ask how we could help protect his safety or influence the state's handling of his incarceration. Having on several prior occasions used my role as therapist to write pre-sentencing letters and offer some degree of expert advice to Judges ahead of their case dispositions, I assumed I could have some control on the family's behalf and for this younger member in particular as well. The assigned prosecutor promptly relieved me of any such delusions of grandeur. I would have no voice or input into any part of the legal process. We as his family would be informed but otherwise only seen and not heard. Period.

Meanwhile, upon returning home to Dayton I felt a new resolve to apply for re-admission to seminary in hopes of taking a class that next Spring semester. I had no idea how many of my credits from 30 years prior, if any, would be accepted in pursuit of my M.Div. degree, but I was prepared to back-track as required in making this new quest for pastoral Christian ministry happen in my future. I remembered the words of Pastor Mike Slaughter from the pulpit, whether he'd ever spoken them or I was only imagining them: Don't retire, but instead recommit, retrain, retool. Don't take care, take charge. Take control. And I was in my own way afraid that not returning to seminary, not pressing on to pastoral ministry, would mean my life was a wasted failure for all eternity. That's how uncertain I was about nearly everything in those days.

By February of 2000 when it came time to return to my seminary we had received news that this younger brother decided to take a plea bargain in his county's courtroom. He would plead guilty of all crimes as charged and agree to serve 3 life-sentences plus 40 years in prison in exchange for their dropping of the death penalty. His wife and her family had accepted these terms, which guaranteed no parole possibilities for him. So we were actually quite relieved to know no other family member would need to die from this horrible crime of that prior October.

In many respects, our lives began to assume some degree of stability in the year to come. Job-wise, both Sue and I felt much stress at work from our respective roles and positions, but we were doing okay. I was enjoying my first seminary class back on campus in the winter of 2000 and would go on to take a couple more courses in the fall.

As driven by my own fear story, one way I sought control over my world again was to take on not one but two part-time jobs within the coming year. I would see some counseling clients at Ginghamsburg Church's New Creation clinic plus I would take on a position with the Sulphur Grove Church near where we lived. I served as Student Associate Pastor of Evangelism there. I developed a close friendship with the lead pastor, Rev. Mike Mahoney, and together with Sue continued serving in marriage ministry around the country with United Marriage Encounter, a non-sectarian Christian retreat ministry for marriages in search of enhanced communication skills and intimacy development. Alongside my full-time job servicing a national psychiatric health maintenance contract, I was too busy to feel any of my own fears. I've since come to regard this as another sign that one's fear story is pushing the envelope closer than ever to a new great awakening. Fear has a way of burning itself out over the course of time.

By September of 2001, I had secured a large enough outside loan that, along with Sue's full-time income, I could leave my clinical jobs, remain part-time with the church, and go full-time with seminary in order to graduate that next May of 2002. The work of grieving over the family incidents out of state had reached some level of acceptance for me, even though our correspondence with both Sue's little brother and surviving sister-in-law would keep emotional tension and uncertainty within my awareness at all times. I never went a day without thinking of them, and in a real sense suffering my own secondary PTSD.

Work in pastoral ministry with my church was beginning to pay some dividends. I was drawn to working with our new lead pastor, Rev. Tom Mellott, in 2001 to develop a program of servant evangelism within our local neighborhoods. I began training with the Cincinnati Vineyard Church ministries under the pastoral leadership of Pastor Steve Sjogren. I had some early success mobilizing teams to do random acts of kindness on the streets of our community as followers of Jesus. No preaching necessary. Just a single sentence with each act of kindness about our "Jesus, whose love is free."

It was what I came to call the orthopraxy of "servant evangelism" that brought me to the summit of my 2nd Great Awakening of God's Spirit. If my infant baptism through my adolescent call to ministry had bathed my 1st Great Awakening in Christian orthodoxy, the 2nd Awakening was closer to a 40-year wilderness wandering finally immersed in Christian orthopraxy. Such a wilderness trek was truly a test of whether my early orthodoxy would serve any practical value or not. Would my faith actually work? Would the certainty born of my earlier faith bear any fruit at all during my times of uncertainty? My encounters with many hundreds of clients such as Nancy and Thomas, the family crises involving violent deaths of children, and many other events too numerous to mention had tested me. And tempted me. Yet, here I was back at United Seminary 30-some years later, working in a "servant evangelism" ministry in my local community, and awakening into Christ's new call into Church-centered ministry.

First time around I became a believer in Jesus as Savior. Second time around I was finally a follower of Jesus as Lord. In so doing, I had journeyed nearly forty years through two deserts of fear emptying into two oases of love. Two very separate Great Awakenings.

What I learned about myself during that long wilderness journey in between spiritual Awakenings was this: when an external event involving "other" people threatens my sense of certainty and security, I become fearful in ways that drive me to "take control over the other" to the best of my ability. This control is but an illusion.

But when most painfully faced with that illusion and my consequential failure to attain such control, I become softened to accept a new truth love has in store for my future. Hence, the fruition of my 2nd Great Awakening as I returned to United Seminary after my 30-year hiatus. It would surely be my last such awakening. I would from this point live out my true love story. Into eternity.

Or so I then imagined.

Then came the fateful morning of Tuesday, September 11, 2001.

CHAPTER SEVEN

Planned detours

"For God has not given us a spirit of fear,
but of power and of love and of a sound mind." -- II Timothy 1:7

While walking between classes at United Seminary on 9/11/01, somewhere around 9:30 a.m., I passed a large screen television in the student center that revealed a shocking scene. A plane had struck the side of the north tower of New York's World Trade Center. Smoke was billowing out of the building. All news reports were at best speculative. This was an "other" experience for both the senders and receivers of this news throughout our nation. No one on either side of the camera, or TV screen, seemed to know what had really happened. I wanted to stay and get more clues about what I was watching. Yet, I went onto my next class as scheduled, after which I decided to make contact with my wife at her place of employment. "Did you see the news, Sue, about the World Trade Center this morning?" *"Yes,"* came her reply. *"I'm watching it right now. Both buildings have been hit by two separate planes. They're giving a report. I'll call you back later."*

Another hour passed.
Sue called me, only with some news much worse than I had ever imagined. It seems she had been trying in vain to contact her other younger brother, Chuck, by phone. He had told her Sunday evening he'd be flying out to LA on Tuesday morning for his Boston-area employer. When he did not answer his cell, she began calling family members. *"Is Chuck okay?"* No one knew for sure. Her own fear turned to panic. More phone calls.
And finally the news.

This younger brother-in-law, Charles ("Chuck") Jones, in so many ways our family hero because of his status as a former U.S. Astronaut in the space shuttle program, a newly retired USAF Colonel now working for BAE Systems, was confirmed as being a passenger on American Airlines FL #11 out of Boston. His was the first plane. The one that exploded into the north side of the North Tower at 8:46 a.m. He was most suddenly gone.

Murder had once again struck among my loved ones, this time with an unforeseen act of international terrorism. And I was once again afraid, seeking control as I rushed to be with my wife at her office, where she was reclined in severe physical distress at the confirmed news of her dear brother's personal terror that morning. The "other" again seemed in control and there was nothing I could do to stop it, to turn back the clock, the calendar, the family. September 11, 2001 was not just happening to other people on the news. It was happening to me. More innocent blood was spilled in our own family. Yet, in this event my old uncertainties had somehow diminished and my new uncertainty had kicked in. I was flooded emotionally with an entirely new uncertainty I'd never known before. In that sense I was then a normal American.

I was back in seminary, already in the throes of what had become my 2nd Great Awakening. Yet, my new certainty was short lived. I was like the doubting Thomas just one week removed from his Lord's own triumphal entry into Jerusalem. Things had gone south in a hurry. The love story I had started again to live out of was already coming unraveled. Its new certainties now were giving way to more fearful uncertainty. My fear story was back to feeling like my life's defining narrative after all. So now what?

Preparation for my 3rd Great Awakening seemed to begin before the proverbial paint from my 2nd awakening had even dried.

Let me try to explain.

My return to seminary was much more satisfying than my first go-round had been. While I never did find out just where Nancy Thomas picked up with her Minnesota family upon return from her prodigal sojourn back in the summer of 1968, I did find out my own prodigal return "home" as part of pastoral education was positive in every respect. After 30 years away from Seminary, I was half-way expecting a place at the far end of the servant's table as assigned in disgrace. While no one threw me any banquets or killed any fatted calves for me, I did find myself in the year 2000 to be a recipient of grace, not disgrace. This had brought me into my 2nd Great Awakening.

Which was nice while it lasted.

Now, after the death of Chuck on 9/11/01, I was reunited with my own pain and grief in ways that left me once again uncertain and afraid. Just when I thought things were falling into place, I was laid low by these latest circumstances. My dear wife, Sue, was still grieving the loss of her other younger brother now imprisoned when Chuck, the sibling she felt the tightest bond with, would die that day aboard American Airlines flight #11. And so my deepest hurt in the grief that followed 9/11 was the hurt my own wife was going through.

In a strange way, Sue had grieved over Chuck for the past five years even before his death. Their bond was such that, for Sue, Chuck's career as a USAF Officer was a kind of vicarious list of achievements she took personal pride in by association. This "little brother" would become the 3rd youngest full Colonel in the Air Force, and had been a career Astronaut as a Manned Spaceflight Engineer for the National Aeronautic Space Administration. Her entire family was well aware of his high level of performance in his field utilizing his MIT graduate degrees in both Astronautical and Aeronautical Engineering after completing undergraduate work at the USAF Academy. But it was only after his death that we came to understand a bit about what had been his own highly classified assignments.

Chuck was originally scheduled as back-up to his training partner, Ellison Onizuka, aboard the Challenger shuttle STS-51-L with a Department of Defense mission in payload. The launch date was set for January 28, 1986.

You're probably already ahead of me in your own mind at this point. Yes, you may even remember the day in question.

That was the flight, and the date, of that ill-fated Challenger shuttle that, amid the freezing temperatures of that morning's Florida space coast, exploded and broke apart 73 seconds after launch. All seven persons aboard were killed. Chuck's training partner, for whom he served as back-up, perished with his crew of 7 astronauts. Chuck, as was then apparent protocol for NASA, was assigned to the next Challenger flight STS-71-B set for December of that same year. However, NASA suffered a tremendous push back in terms of both national media and industrial re-design such that his own flight, scheduled for late in 1986, would be forever cancelled, and with enormous disappointment on Chuck's part due to the rigors of astronaut training over the prior 11 years of his Air Force career. All manned space launches were scrubbed by NASA for the ensuing 32-month period (http://cancelled-space-shuttle-missions.wikia.com/wiki/STS-71-B) including Chuck's promised launch in December, 1986.

While remaining as a Colonel with high-level responsibilities for satellite intelligence administration during the 1990's, his career plateaued in such a way as to bring about an early retirement for him late in that decade, and a new civilian career with BAE systems as a space mission contractor at the time of his death. The project he was managing for them out in Los Angeles placed him frequently on that American AL flight #11 from Boston.

The trauma of September 11, 2001 for Sue took her literally to a local hospital emergency room as she experienced, soon after the news of Chuck's demise, a pain in the back of her head that was excruciating in its intensity. Her CT scan revealed no physical damage, but it is uncertain how her pain may have been psychologically connected with her dear brother's own physical trauma at the point of death upon impact with the first WTC tower. Stranger things have happened, I surmised, connecting a physical and psychological trauma between siblings.

As a husband, this was a time for many of my own growing pains in our marriage. I would observe Sue's reactions during that first year after 9/11 each time the TV would, amidst our broader national time of mourning, replay the events of that day at the World Trade Center. Obsessed as the news media seemed with finding film footage of the planes hitting the towers, the fire and smoke spreading about, the towers collapsing, Sue was struggling with the help of her own counseling to grasp the "why?" of that entire tragedy on the heels of other recent critical losses in her life, including those in October of 1999. Now with Chuck's sudden and senseless death, her hurt was magnified. As Chuck's family hurt, so did Sue. As Sue hurt, so did I.

The first thing to most naturally follow hurt is fear. Hurt is the spark that ignites the flames of fear. From there, we naturally move into anger even as fire moves into smoke. Indeed, given that analogy, there are times when all we can see resulting from the spark of hurt or the flames of fear will be the anger that often resembles black clouds of smoke overhead.

Anger within our human relationships can drive us to take control, one way or another. Sometimes control means taking flight, running away, or even going into denial. Think back to the disciples of Jesus after his crucifixion. They were in flight mode behind locked doors soon to follow the Friday events. Or take his most famous disciple, Simon Peter. He was in denial mode from the time of Jesus's arrest, thinking only of his own safety.   He was taking control of an out of control situation in the only way he then knew how.

Another way in which we often take control when most afraid of the hurtful situation at hand is by going into some mode of fight that projects all blame upon the "other" found at the scene.   We then say and do hurtful things to others we would not normally do under other circumstances.   We are thus prone to fulfill the old adage, "hurt people hurt people."   We can easily hurt, scare, and even infuriate other people at such times.   We can have in mind, at a typically unconscious level, more faith in fear than we have in love, seeming to reverse the promise of Paul to young Timothy when he wrote, *"For God has not given us a spirit of fear, but of power and of love and of a sound mind."*   -- II Timothy 1:7

The seeds of my 3rd Great Awakening were the very fears and hurts Sue and I, and the rest of her family, shared.   Within three years of the Challenger explosion in 1986, my Father-in-law died of a heart attack.   Ten years later my other younger brother-in-law was guilty of those horrible murders, then came 9/11, and within another six months the death of my wife's mother.   Soon to be followed by another job loss for Sue, the death of two dear family pets, and her own acute episode of Major Depression.   We both used more than our share of fight or flight, denial or projection, in our marriage during these awful months following 9/11.   Only our love built upon 34 years of holy matrimony, and God's own perfect love and grace, would see us through these times.

How God sees us through our times of crisis, such as our family experienced after 9/11, often involves sending someone special into our lives to help make sense of things.   For me, one such person was a theology professor I had then in seminary.   He helped me find new meaning in suffering.   His name is Andrew Park.   To think that Dr. Park had in his own theological studies achieved any perfect understanding of God's love would be wrong, yet to me he embodied one moving on to such perfection better than perhaps anyone else I'd met before in my then 55 years on earth.   He, more than anyone else I knew, seemed to embody that very Wesleyan or Methodist hope for God's grace unto perfection.

Dr. Park introduced me to his native Korean concept of *han* through his expertise in the "*Minjung* theology" of Minjung Sinhak in South Korea.   *Han* itself refers to an ages old Korean concept of struggle for justice in the face of overwhelming odds. Its historical roots are found within the Korean peninsula upon recurrent invasions over the course of several centuries by "other" nations seeking control over its land and seas. The Korean people themselves were seen as a type of collateral damage by their captors, often scapegoated as innocent victims to be sacrificially removed for the sake of their conquering invaders. They were perpetual victims of this invasive injustice over the centuries. As such, their concept of *han* as the struggle for justice would lead many in Dr. Park's homeland, himself included, to embrace Jesus as the one whose resurrection had effectively completed God's own struggle for justice. Jesus saves us from the world's control over us and restores us to justice.

Now my words about this are not necessarily the *Minjung* understanding of God's justice-winning love through Jesus Christ. At least they are not according to Dr. Park's own exact words. But they became my own new understanding of the relationship resurrection itself would have with the human experience of fear. It would be an empowering relationship worth exploring further. In resurrection, love will have power over fear. Justice will win the struggle against injustice. In love's resurrection, fear's heaviest of stones is rolled away. Yet, there can be no resurrection apart from that suffering of crucifixion and injustice.

Just as God used Dr. Park to help me find meaning and healing during my post-9/11 suffering, so God sends someone special into all our lives to help make sense of things. That's where Jesus comes in, whose crucifixion was the worst possible *han* and injustice, but whose resurrection was our ultimate hope of victory and best possible justice.

In one of my favorite Thornton Wilder plays, "The Angel That Troubled the Water," a conclusion is reached in which the wounded invalids seeking healing for themselves are able to finally help each other in ways even the assigned angels could not alone accomplish. Why? Because in love's service, only wounded hearts can qualify. From such a moving scene in earthly drama came my own new grasp of God's personal love story, in which he becomes the wounded and crucified Christ who heals in ways the Holy Spirit alone could not accomplish. What then culminates in the new reality of God's Kingdom on earth is that, instead of hurt people hurting people, we find hurt people most uniquely, and powerfully, helping people.

The apostle Paul served God's Kingdom well in just such a capacity. He used his own afflictions as a source of comfort for others, noting that Christ's afflictions were the prior source of his own comfort. The new covenant in Jesus Christ was marked for Paul as being God's way of turning hurt into help. Here is how Paul put it upon writing his second letter to the Corinthians: "*Blessed be the God and Father of our Lord Jesus Christ, the Father of mercies and the God of all consolation, who consoles us in all our affliction, so that we may be able to console those who are in any affliction with the consolation with which we ourselves are consoled by God. For just as the sufferings of Christ are abundant for us, so also our consolation is abundant through Christ. If we are being afflicted, it is for your consolation and salvation; if we are being consoled, it is for your consolation, which you experience when you patiently endure the same sufferings that we are also suffering. Our hope for you is unshaken; for we know that as you share in our sufferings, so also you share in our consolation.*" -- 2 Corinthians 1:3-7. In other words, God blesses hurt people to help other hurting people. The Korean Christians are following in this precise path in today's world.

Near the end of my seminary work, I would take one more course from Dr. Park, using the inspiration of his own Korean *han* to help fill out some of the systematic theology that would lead in the direction of my own 3rd Great Awakening.

In the next three chapters, I will share something of what I found to be more faithful or trustworthy in my own mind as I spell out three segments of my theology having to do with God, with Sin, and with Salvation. This new system of explaining my faith even to myself would form the basis for the last of my Great Awakenings to date. From this new base I would discover my truer life story and the most recent love story in which I am now still living.

By way of warning, readers from this point forward will be exposed to much controversy. I will be dealing with some concepts that might seem strange or at least new. And there will be many temptations to resist my own very different ways of looking at God, sin, and salvation. What follows may test the most open-minded of readers.

CHAPTER EIGHT

God

"In the beginning God created the heavens and the earth." --
Genesis 1:1

*"In the beginning was the Word, and the Word was with God,
and the Word was God."* -- John 1:1

Great Awakenings having to do with religious or spiritual changes are lodged in the human psyche. By this I mean, we have a major change of mind, a new way of thinking and understanding about God and/or the world around us. We have a new faith. We adopt a new paradigm.

Such a paradigm shift may be labeled "Great" if involving a conscious transformation from people of great faith in fear to an even greater faith in love. This is true both on a personal and communal level, the latter experienced when by some mysteriously critical mass, enough minds have been changed to create a culture shift in the area of faith paradigms.

As has already been recounted, America's Great Awakenings have occurred over a period of years rather than days. Just as it takes time to turn an aircraft carrier at sea, so it takes time to shift the course of public opinion. Communal problems have a rather long gestation period leading up to the birth of our solutions. On the problem end, what I'm calling "faith in fear" as our nation's dominant narrative builds ever so gradually over a period of years. This triggers a crisis. Fear grows to a point where it cannot sustain itself, collapsing under its own weight. Like a butterfly emerging from a chrysalis, we awaken to a new love story that overcomes those old fears. We live out of our newly awakened love story for a period to come. Only to then cycle back into a gradual process of fear triggered by some new traumatic world event. Stressors serve as tempters and triggers, human minds thus having a tendency to regress from a new faith in love back to an old faith in fear. It's a back and forth dance between two competing faith narratives. One containing some truth but the other much more truth in the mind's own judgment.

What we might call psychic equilibrium is really the mind's

own balance between faith and doubt. Even the national psyche maintains a level of faith vs. doubt. We rock back and forth between faith in fear but doubt in love and its counter-balanced opposite.

As real as this seems to me concerning the America I live in, it has also been my own reality at a personal level. By age 18, with my call to pastoral ministry, I'd grounded myself in what I then considered as my truest life story, a love story, that would last forever. I now call that my 1st Great Awakening. Yet by age 22, I'd already regressed into a fear story that caused me to leave behind my seminary education and follow a somewhat different career path. Then, at age 52, having experienced a crisis point in that same incremental fear story, I found myself seeking and finding a higher level of love than ever before upon the long-awaited resumption of my seminary degree. Calling that my 2nd Great Awakening, it then seemed as if I'd stepped back into a permanent love story. I was again living a new narrative of faith that cast doubt upon all the fears I'd built up over the prior 30 years culminating in that loss of illusory *control* the year before. Little did I then know I would soon require a 3rd Great Awakening in my life.

Keeping in mind that because heightened fear always motivated me to seek some *control over the other* which then proved to be an illusion or a fool's errand into the impossible, I could only fail forward. By that I mean, having failed to take *control* over the uncertain world around me that fear had demanded I do, I then doubted fear's reality enough to form a deeper faith in the reality of love. Love would demand no such *unrealistic control* over any other. It would invite me to offer only *what influence I could.* And that would become my new truth, one I hoped would last forever.

If you haven't caught on by now, such hope or even faith in love has not, at any level, seemed to last forever. It instead gives way to more fear again, as was true when Chuck was killed on 9/11 and our entire nation descended into a fear of terrorism. As that fear builds, however, it reaches another crisis stage in which *control* is again attempted, again fails, and a newer and truer love story is again resurrected. These next three chapters will dwell in this more recent period of faith in love that I call my 3rd Great Awakening.

Leading into my most recent awakening, I have struggled with my own fears. I will share more about these in the next chapter, but as always these fears have to do with future uncertainties. From

2000 to the present, my fears have danced about with my own love story but the lead has more recently switched. Now love is in the lead. My faith is now in love, and my doubt is more in the direction of fear itself.

And my faith in love begins with God.

As with the course in Systematic Theology I now recall from my final year of seminary (I didn't finish my M.Div. until May of 2002), God is always the best place to begin. So as my own mind has worked through the fears and doubts of these first years in the new millennia, I have wrestled with my own question of What is God and Who is God.

I've crossed paths with some people over these years who indeed think of God as a What rather than a Who. For them God constitutes a divine *essence*, but that *essence* has no *existence*. To them God might represent, for example, the essence of *Love*. Yet, God would not have the existence of an actual *Lover*.

I've always rejected such a notion as these very well-meaning people have advanced. To me there can be no love without a lover. And there can be no *essence* without an *existence*. If there is an essential *what*, there must be a *who* when it comes to either human or divine existence. And this is especially true where love is concerned. Love cannot be without becoming. Love requires a lover. For me, in my own thought process, it has to have a "who" if there is any such 'what." Essence requires existence as nouns require verbs.

By the same token, it would be impossible for my own mind to conceive of a lover if there were no love to begin with. No "who" without such a "what." *No existence without an essence.* To the atheists and humanists I've met along my journey, the essence of love requires only human existence. They see no need and certainly no evidence for a higher existence. This is not the time to in any way debate their logic. Rather, I'm only attempting to now speak my own mind. I don't assume or otherwise expect others to agree with my own thinking here, or elsewhere on these pages.

I've also crossed paths over these recent decades with those who think of God as being up there or out there and totally beyond where you and I are now. Some theologians apply the word *transcendence* to their own understanding of a God totally beyond us. Some say God is *wholly other* with respect to God's essence and/or existence. Taken to the extreme, this denies or at least minimizes God's presence here and now within you and me. Or what theologians like to call God's *immanence*.

My own mind has rejected this notion of God's transcendence as insufficient. To me, if God is transcendent, then God is big enough to be fully present here and now within you and me. In other words, *God is both transcendent and immanent*. God is both *there* and *here*, both *height* and *depth*. *God is both essence and existence*. God is both a *what* and a *who*. That's how I've learned to think of God over the years.

When I speak of my seminary years in particular, I should clarify for any who may not know that United Seminary is a United Methodist school representing what is often labeled as mainline Protestant Christianity. And mainline Protestant thinking about God is no different than Catholic and Orthodox Christianity when it comes to affirming God as being and becoming. God has both essence and existence in all three of these most common Christian traditions. For that matter, these traditions all speak in some sense of God's Trinity. Beyond the mainline churches of Protestantism, there are non-Trinitarian images of God. But I was trained to explore and understand God more in terms of the Trinity of Father, Son, and Holy Spirit, most often spoken of in that order.

The United Methodist tradition within this larger mainline Protestant tradition, has its own approach to questions of faith and doubt. If to the casual observer of Christianity most things seem to happen in threes, please note that for Methodists they happen in fours. Or at least this is so in the matter of something we call the Quadrilateral.

Let me explain.

John Wesley, the principal founder of Methodist Christianity was an Anglican Priest in England. And from his own seminary and pastoral background, he based his own systematic theology upon four points of authority. The first was the Bible. So he studied what was in the Christian scriptures to find answers to his faith questions. The other three points involved reason, experience and tradition. For Wesley, reason itself rested with not only the scripture as could be studied and thought through, but also one's personal experience and communal tradition. He saw no way to have faith without reason, and no way to interpret scripture or experience or even tradition apart from reason. The head, the brain if you will, would have to participate or there could be no faith. Indeed, without reason there could be no understanding of authoritative scripture, private experience, or public tradition. Methodism, then, was itself lodged within the human psyche. If reason failed to participate, accounting for both subjective emotions and objective traditions, then the scriptures lacked any actual authority. Reason would have to take the lead before faith could fully mature or become awakened.

What follows in these next pages, then, is my own current state of reasoning about God based on the authority of scripture combined with my private experience and public tradition. You will notice that tradition is much less privileged than experience when it comes to my 3rd awakening notions of God as you read on from this point.

The scripture itself begins with these words, *"In the beginning, God...."* The scripture, which was written only by men, no women, accounted for many of the core stories told about God among the ancient Hebrew people. Or at least their male members. So it uses only a masculine language to define God. I have no such definition in mind when thinking of God, but for ease of explaining my broader ideas about God I will continue here to use masculine pronouns in referencing my 3rd Great Awakening. I will, somewhat grudgingly here, privilege tradition above experience. I will refer to God in the masculine as I continue this writing.

The book of Genesis tells two distinct creation stories (in the ancient Hebrew language). The stories come from two separate sources, aiming to explain the ancient Mesopotamian creation mythology but with only one creator deity. The first of these two stories contained in Genesis 1 reveals that deity's name as being *Elohim* who "speaks" the world into being. Genesis 2 reveals that same deity's name to be *Yahweh* who "breathes" life into being. Each creates in a different order. And while they represent two separate sources (*Priestly* and *Jahwist*) among the ancient Hebrews, they may in at least my own mind represent two rather different parts within the same whole we as Christians call the *Godhead*.

The first, *Elohim*, represents for my own awakened understanding, the body by which God speaks forth creation. John's Gospel writer in the New Testament asserted his own understanding that this body was Jesus Christ. *"In the beginning was the Word, and the Word was with God, and the Word was God"* (John 1:1). So there is some biblical correlation between Genesis 1 and John 1 to at least consider and reasonably account for.

The second, *Yahweh*, represents for me the soul, the Spirit, by which God breathes forth creation.

Genesis 1 reveals a God whose Spirit or wind (as translated from the Hebrew *ruach*) at first *"hovered over the surface of the waters"* in verse 2, followed by a God who speaks *"let there be light,"* who then names the light *"day."* Then God names the darkness *"night,"* before going on to speak into existence and name sequentially the water, sky, land, vegetation, sun, stars, fish, birds, then animals of every kind and function, before settling in on the creation of humanity to rule over the prior creation. This embodied God has voice, and that voice has creative power.

Minor as it may seem to others, I consider it highly significant that the first appearance on the biblical creation stage was not God, the speaker. Rather, it was God the Spirit. Call it trivial pursuit on my part, but I find it biblically relevant that the *ruach* enters in verse 2 prior to any actual spoken work of creation in verse 3. If the Spirit works at all, it is by mere whisper or wind or breath. The Spirit alone is considered to be void and without form. Or I would prefer to think of it as form without function, perhaps also essence without existence. God in Genesis 1:1-2 is a noun without a verb. Then comes 1:3 when the verbs of actual creation have their, well, genesis.

This, for my part, suggests further evidence that the Spirit is God's essence in search of existence. God's form in search of function. And that function being altogether relational. This first biblical creation story about Elohim culminates in Genesis 1:27, *"So God created man in his own image; he created him in the image of God; he created them male and female."* Here God functions to then form a new relationship, which he calls good. That first biblical creation story ends on that good note. Yet, what helps make it good is that we human creatures are said to actually mirror God. God declares in 1:26, *"Let us make man in our image, according to our likeness."* Notice the *"us"* and *"our"* in this text derives from the Hebrew word for God, *Elohim*, which is in plural form. Whether such an *"us"* involves *"male and female"* is perhaps best left to conjecture, but were such a motion on the floor I would gladly second it just to get the discussion rolling.

To me, the greater implication of God's plural self-image has to do with functionality more than sexuality. To explain, I now from my own 3rd Great Awakening believe the "us" and "our" of 1:26 to mean God's body that speaks, spirit that breathes, and mind that decides. This is the 3-in-1 of God's Holy and Triune image; the same image in which we, too, are created. So in my own reading of the first creation story, I infer within my own mind that God's body does the work of creation while God's soul, or Spirit, does the hovering above as something of a perhaps "higher power."

Then this same *ruach* Spirit, however, breathes creation of human life into existence in Genesis 2:7 before adding the featured vegetation and animal life that would then support our human existence. Both God's body and soul may be reasonably inferred as present at creation, forming at least a duality if not a trinity. Again, the priestly word for God in Hebrew, *Elohim*, is the plural for *El* even though, by all accounts, the priestly source was emphatically aimed at a monotheistic explanation of creation. So God is One, not three, just as you and I are one, not three, despite having our own body, mind, and soul carrying out three unique functions.

To recap, then, we have two distinct creation stories in the Bible, the Genesis 1 creation being performed by God's body through speaking while in Genesis 2 it was performed by God's soul through breathing. My inference: God is both body and soul (duality). Yet, there is a third part of God quite implicit within both of these early stories. God appears to have a mind that evaluates good vs. bad and decides among categorical options that form an ecosystem as needed to support human life. Hence, the communal tradition of addressing God as Trinity (in this case God's mind, body, and soul). Deconstructing that triune image for God a bit further, I address this Trinity as Father (God's mind), Son (God's body), and Holy Spirit (God's soul).

To the Methodist foundations of scripture, reason and tradition, I also would add my own "experience" as a person in my own part, reportedly created in God's same image.

Here's what that means to me.

As I do the work of understanding God, or deconstructing the "what" and "who" of God, what I experience is an understanding of my own *essence* and *existence*, my own triune image being that of a mind, body, and soul as created by God's mind, body, and soul in the Genesis stories.

So how do "these" three in one work together in my own life? And how might these reflect upon God's primary image? To such a question, I begin by considering my mind's decision processes.

How, for instance, does my mind go about deciding in matters of fear and love? Inside my own 3rd Great Awakening, I understand my fear to come about through my body informing my mind and demanding its decision to take control. Given the uncertainties of the world in which my body is affected, my bodily senses and emotions indirectly communicate the world to my mind. The extent to which the world seems chaotic and out of control is the extent to which my body demands that my mind take control over this chaotic world around me. Fortunately, the world is not always in chaos and so my bodily senses inform my mind of more pleasant certainties than painful uncertainties over all. Sometimes, though, the world can change rather quickly, moving order into chaos in ways that produce intense fear in body and mind.

Here is an example of how that works. It involves a near tragedy that happened many years ago while Sue and I were spending a leisurely Sunday afternoon at Ohio's Cowan Lake State Park. This man-made 700-acre reservoir had a small boat livery, so we rented a canoe and threw in our blanket, picnic lunch, and a deck of cards. Paddled to a small cove on the opposite side of the lake and went ashore in a nice wooded, quiet cove. There we were shaded not only from the sun but from the clouds that began forming overhead. When we finally noticed the clouds forming in mid-afternoon, we began feeling afraid. We feared getting soaked there if a rain storm should arrive. We rather hurriedly packed up and headed to shore on the other side.

But we had a problem.

We had waited a bit too long and were only about half-way across that 700-acre lake when the water started to become choppy. Very choppy. The sky was turning dark. Very dark. Here came the wind. Then the thunder and soon lightning that was bouncing off the lake's surface. Then some nearby strikes probably no more than 100 feet away. The rain was pouring down on us. Soon the shoreline was no longer visible to us.

As husband and wife, we have a hard enough time rowing a straight line across a lake when the water is calm owing to our limited experience with canoes. So by this point on that stormy afternoon, there was no crossing of the lake in this rented aluminum craft. No forward progress could be had, even if we could've seen the shore to know which way "forward" even was.

To say we were afraid at that time would be a marked

understatement. Try "terrified."

Never before in life had I ever been so doubtful of my own survival. I started believing this was probably the end. I was going to die. Yes, we were wearing life vests. But, no, we had no expectation this aluminum canoe with us as the tallest objects in the water during a lightning storm would keep us alive even if we did manage to keep the canoe upright within the bouncing waves.

Here is what I learned about my own mind in those moments that seemed like hours. My mind's choices and decisions were informed by two very conflicted voices within.

Let me explain.

My body was shouting at me to take control and get this boat ashore asap! My body's heightened senses and increased adrenaline were driving panic into my mind's thought process that demanded me to keep rowing. Sue's body was informing her mind in that same exact way. Together we were working our hardest to get ashore.

Yet, there was another voice I had in mind in those moments. More of a whisper than a shout. And I've come to believe it was my soul. Instead of this voice "driving panic" into my mind, it was like a deeper breath "drawing peace" into my mind's thought process. Instead of demanding me to keep rowing in order to get ashore, it was desiring me to start relaxing in order to stay afloat. Oars in the water to achieve balance, yes. Oars in motion to attempt progress, no. That was my soul's advice to my mind quite opposite my body's advice. Work smarter, not harder. Forget forward progress. Float with the waves.

Though it seemed like a long time that we were bouncing around in this little canoe upon a big lake in an even bigger storm, oars only resting in water for balance, Sue and I were finally spotted by a lone man in a motor boat. He alone was out there on that 700-acre lake under conditions of short visibility. He somehow was there to see us, and to come and tie on to us and motor us to shore safely that day. He literally saved our lives. Yet, when we arrived, lugging our canoe and soaked belongings ashore to the rental livery counter, we turned around and could not find him anywhere to even thank. To this day, the man who saved us is unknown to us. But we are still just as saved as if we had gotten his picture, name, and even mailing address. A total stranger had rescued us because we had obeyed our soul's deep breath of desire and relaxed just enough to stay afloat where we could be miraculously spotted and rescued.

This traumatic experience came to make particular sense to me much later on amidst my own 3rd Great Awakening. It reminded me that my mind itself is never alone. My mind has two constant companions, one being my body and one my soul. They don't always agree or see things the same way. Both act to inform my mind's decisions. Together they function to create my reality and to shape the story into which I will live.

Such a process has shaped, even transformed, my understanding of God within my 3rd Great Awakening. It has also caused me to place my greatest faith in not only my own truer love story but in God as its truest source. What emerges from that experience at sea within my own mind's reasoning is that I now believe my inner soul has access to a higher power than what my body and mind can grasp on their own. Hence, my own doubt in atheism and humanism.

When in second Isaiah 55:8 we read *"For my thoughts are not your thoughts, nor are your ways my ways, says the LORD,"* I'm understanding the prophet to suggest God's thoughts, feelings and actions are primary while our own are secondary and thus separated in sequence. That is, God's thoughts and ways are before and above ours. A prior and higher power is involved. So in Isaiah 55:9 the prophet adds, *"For as the heavens are higher than the earth, so are my ways higher than your ways and my thoughts than your thoughts."*

The biblical story of Moses and the burning bush found in Exodus 3 is one where God embodies himself as a visible angel speaking with an audible voice from within a burning bush. Elsewhere God speaks not only through material objects but mostly through embodied humans who the Hebrews called Prophets. The Hebrew word, *navi*, meaning *"spokesperson,"* is used to describe how God opens his mouth and speaks through these Prophetic messengers. The writer of Deuteronomy 18:18 acts out this prophetic role by quoting God as saying, *"and I will put my words in his mouth, and he shall speak unto them all that I shall command him."* Isaiah serving as one such *navi* in the Old Testament thus implies that although God said his ways and thoughts are higher than ours, God lowers himself into human form for the sake of revelation or communication. So God is far more than just a disembodied spirit watching over us. God not only knows but also cares. God not only creates all but also communicates with all creatures. And that communication takes the form of an "embodied" spirit, the Word becoming flesh (John 1:14).

That said, there are some who understand the Hebrew word, *nephesh*, within our Old Testament scriptures to reference a disembodied Spirit of God. The other Hebrew word for Spirit, *ruach*, is more clearly a reference to God's Holy Spirit within our own bodies, an example being King David's references within Psalm 139. Here again, I tend to believe in both the soul as a life in *essence* and the body as a life in *existence*. One is merely being, while the other is actively doing and becoming. Neither is complete without the other.

I have then carried over from the Hebrew Bible to the New Testament stories concerning Jesus this same image. In my most awakened mind to date, God reveals himself to be the body of Jesus acting in accord with the mind of his Father and the soul of his Holy Spirit. God enjoys the capacity to think, feel, and act in relationship with humanity. God knows and God cares. God embodies himself in humanity for the sake of communicating in helpful ways. God sees our problems on earth and acts to help solve them, not by directly controlling them but rather by indirectly influencing them.

Which brings me to the concept of love.

The Old Testament uses three or four words to describe love, but two in particular stand out in terms of God's love. The Hebrew word *ahab* seems, if I understand it correctly, to embody love and give it a bodily component in relationship. It's a kind of body to body love, if you will. The other word *hesed*, on the contrary, seems to be more about a spiritual power transacted soul to soul. God's mind strikes me throughout the Old Testament as choosing to use both according to the situation at hand.

Let me at least try to explain my new thinking here.

Biblical scholars may consider this an unfair comparison, but within my own mind's 3rd Great Awakening, I've come to compare the *ahab* love more with our own English experience of "to like" another. God, for instance, often did like people. Often, but not always! And when God could not "like" the Hebrew people as in *ahab*, God would "love" the people as in *hesed*. The latter refers to times when God's steadfast love and faithfulness and loyalty extends through God's "higher thoughts" or higher power to love even those he sometimes dislikes.

This shift from like to love, *ahab* to *hesed* in the biblical
Hebrew, involves a change of God's mind. This is evidenced by
another Hebrew word, *naham*, that means repent, relent, or
otherwise shift one's thinking from the more physical liking, or
disliking, of another to the higher and more powerful spiritual
loving, indeed forgiving, of another.

Who of us has not drawn from some capacity (I call it
spiritual or a "higher power" within) to love someone in our lives
even when we thoroughly dislike them for something that was said
or done or both? Could that someone even be a spouse or other
family member? As I own such an experience within my own life, I
find it reasonable to take the scriptural image of God's love and note
my own bodily *ahab* for others as often less enduring than my prior
and higher spiritual *hesed* for others whom I may not always
physically like. By that same imagery, I find my more enduring and
steadfast *hesed* "love" for those I don't particularly *ahab* "like" now
informing my mind's decisions quite separately. This results when I
draw from "God's higher power" within me.

Another way to think of this is the difference, and resulting
conflict, between conditional love for some, our human *ahab,* and
unconditional love for all, God's divine *hesed.*

Here, then, is a key point within my 3rd Great Awakening: my
mind is at times heavily conflicted between my body that shouts
fearful information and my soul that whispers loving information to
affect my mind's next decision. It is a conflict or competition
between low and high, world and heaven, fear and love. My body
speaks the language of conditional love (*ahab*) as if to advise the
mind, "have faith in fear, for you know you don't always like them."
Meanwhile, my soul speaks the language of unconditional love
(*hesed*)as if to advise my mind: "have faith in love, for you know
you can always love them even when you don't like them." My
mind must then decide between these two opposing advisers.

Have you ever noticed your own mind experiencing a similar
kind of conflict?

Then consider Jesus, as depicted in the New Testament of
scripture.

Jesus, though describing himself as the Son of Man, also is
quoted often within the fourth Gospel, as having a unique
relationship with God whom he calls Father. One interesting point
within all four Gospels is that God directly calls Jesus Son not by

birth but by baptism ((MT 3:17, MK 1:11, LK 3:22, JN 1:34). But later on in John's Gospel, in chapter 14, we read of a kind of Question and Answer session with his disciples where Jesus explains that he is in the Father and the Father is in him. No longer is the Father just a voice from heaven. In Jesus the Father is now here. In this way, the heavenly Father becomes perfectly visible and audible and relatable. Want to know what God is like? Know what Jesus is like. *"If you know me, you will know my Father also. From now on you do know him and have seen him"* (John 14:7). Jesus goes on, *"Do you not believe that I am in the Father and the Father is in me? The words that I say to you I do not speak on my own; but the Father who dwells in me does his works. Believe me that I am in the Father and the Father is in me; but if you do not, then believe me because of the works themselves"* (14:10-11).

To me, such scripture suggests an image of Jesus and the Father much like that of a body and mind. The Father is the decider and the Son, Jesus, is the actor. If John's high Christology is to be believed, then we may well find God's own divine mind operating within this human body of Jesus. Jesus, as body, informs his mind's decisions in part, but the Father, as mind itself, actually makes the final decisions. Unlike the rest of us, the body of Jesus had the Father for a mind. His Father was always in accord with his soul (Holy Spirit) so, while listening to the body's advice, the final decision always came down to the soul's higher and heavenly advice.

What the Gospels then tell us is that Jesus desired for his disciples to have this same body-mind relationship with the Father and this same mind-soul relationship with the Holy Spirit.

Which brings us back to that Q & A session John is writing about in his 14th chapter. There, Jesus says, *"And I will ask the Father, and he will give you another Advocate to be with you forever. This is the Spirit of truth, whom the world cannot receive, because it neither sees him nor knows him. You know him, because he abides with you, and he will be in you"* (14:16-17). To me this suggests that Jesus was so identified with a divine trinity that, while his role was to speak after the Father first decided the words, together they would give their own soul to us. It stands to reason, then, in my own mind that God is One person, whose *essence* (what is God?) is the soul (Holy Spirit) but whose *existence* (who is God?) is the mind (Father) and body (Son). And that we, created in the same image by the will and decision of this same heavenly Father, bear our own unique body and mind while also housing God's one common soul. It is this third part of us that is forever. Our human body and mind are but a mortal Temple to be one day torn down.

Given that my own Trinitarian understanding of God may seem to escape any reasoning based on communal tradition within the western church, I must add that in addition to my personal experience referencing such times as my canoe adventure on Lake Cowan cited earlier, I do have a scripture that strikes me as more authoritative than perhaps anything else. It is found in Matthew 28, the one chapter I find best illustrates the dueling narratives of fear and love our minds are all challenged to choose between for ourselves. The chapter closes with these words from Christ's "Great Commission" as the church has traditionally named them: *"And Jesus came and said to them, 'All authority in heaven and on earth has been given to me. Go therefore and make disciples of all nations, baptizing them in the name of the Father and of the Son and of the Holy Spirit, and teaching them to obey everything that I have commanded you. And remember, I am with you always, to the end of the age'"* (Matthew 28:18-20). This is the closest either Christ's disciples Matthew or John ever come to naming God's Trinity for our understanding. Jesus Christ appears to understand this Trinity in the context of baptism, wherein we all, made in this same image, are crucified in body and resurrected in soul according to the will and decision of the mind to which we surrender. Having accomplished all three, Jesus shares in our resurrection as the One soul that is with us always, to the end of the age.

So now onto a somewhat different, perhaps even stranger, question. Why would I consider Jesus to be fully human as well as fully divine other than his own often repeated label for himself as Son of Man also in the pages of scripture? If I'm claiming he is, in effect, 2/3 divine in mind and soul and only 1/3 human in body, why not just say Jesus was some embodied angel more along the lines of those ancient Gnostics?

I think of two particular stories from scripture that reveal the fully human embodiment of God in Jesus Christ, if you will grant me some further space for explanation in this now perhaps tiring chapter. These stories tell of Jesus's very own fear story and its human struggle for control within his own earthly life. Both of these stories suggest to me a very real conflict in relation to God's own preferred love narrative. Even Jesus was subject to fear's dominant story for his life from time to time.

The first of these times is revealed in that familiar story of wilderness temptations. We find this story both in Matthew 4 and Luke 4, but I will attend now to the one from Matthew because of some essential, I believe, differences concerning the order of these three temptations in question.

Many scholars far more advanced than me privilege Matthew's ordering because he uses the Greek *tote* meaning "then" to reference the sequence of temptations in this story, while Luke uses the Greek *kai* meaning "and" to perhaps imply the sequence itself didn't really matter. In any case, I will attempt to signify the impact Matthew's ordering of these temptations has within my 3rd Great Awakening. To me, Matthew's story in sequence really does matter.

The first temptation of Jesus in the wilderness was for food. Resonates with most of us who have experienced a desire for food before. Haven't we all? But this temptation was not about desire. It was about fear. Fear of starvation. Desire is about getting what we want. Fear is about not getting what we need, in this case meaning his own survival. After sufficient time without, Jesus's desire turned to fear. And so the temptation to *"tell these stones to become bread"* (MT 4:3) spoke not to the wants in his life but to the needs. That, to me, is a profound difference.

The things we want in life provide what I call lighter temptations of desire. But the things we need in life provide what I call heavier temptations of fear. A need, or necessity, is something we cannot do without. Our wants in this world may be frustrated when interfered with, but to interfere with our needs brings fear even to the point of panic.

The humanist school of psychology, perhaps best represented by Dr. Abraham Maslow, helps us understand a sequence or hierarchy of human needs that corresponds perhaps with no coincidence to Matthew's ordering of the wilderness temptations for Jesus. Our heaviest level of need is for safety and survival. Take away our food, our air, our water supply, etc. and we experience abnormal fear. Make that anxiety. Panic. Not just normal desire. At that point, the temptation to do anything for the sake of our survival is well past mild or medium desire to the point of severe demand: *"tell these stones to become bread."* This is how fear begged for control in Jesus's own life.

The second temptation according to Matthew was "*throw yourself down*" from the "*pinnacle of the temple*" (MT 4: 5-6) in line with what Maslow might call our human need for security. Being claimed as God's *beloved Son* days earlier upon his baptism, surely God would secure his landing. Fear of not at least attempting that leap involved a threat to Jesus's own need to trust in his perpetual security. Surely God would save his own beloved Son, but he needed to know for absolute certain what he could trust in for his own security. Right? Why not test God just to make sure? In any case, our need for future security extends beyond our human need for immediate survival and presents its own set of temptations us as we each journey through this life. Jesus, per self-report concerning his wilderness experiences (no one else was there to record or report for him), was no exception.

The third temptation was then for Jesus "*to fall down and worship me* [devil]*, and I will give you all the kingdoms of the world and their splendor*" (MT 4:8-9). This falls in line with what some in humanist psychology might call our human need for status. Others might call this our need for social belonging or at the very least "social acceptance." In any case, to have such a promise of status only to lose out on the opportunity could well have struck fear into the fully human Jesus in that wilderness experience. Given the promise of social belonging and status, to pass up this opportunity would have been for Jesus like you or me passing up an offer for our dream job or dream house or both. Fear of never again getting such an offer or promise created its own temptation.

What did Jesus do? When afraid of potentially unmet needs for safety, survival, and status, his body informed his mind accordingly. In response, the mind's apparent answer as decided by the Father was essentially "no, no, and no." Jesus then speaks for the Father in using "reason based on scriptural authority" when saying, no because "*man must not live on bread alone but on every word that comes from the mouth of God*" (DT 8:3). And then, no because "*do not test the Lord your God*" (DT 6:6). And finally, no because "*you must worship the Lord your God, and serve only him*" (DT 6:13). Jesus, however anxious he may have been within his own body, obediently told the devil what his soul supplied for his mind's use in deciding the answers.

The devil Jesus encountered was, I believe, his own fear story.

A story based on lies and an invitation to trust in his own fear; placing doubt, then, in his own love story.

I wonder if the same is not true for each one of us as well.

We, too, are in some ways conflicted as to where to place our faith and our doubt when facing tomorrow's uncertainties. We, too, are confronted by the devil of our own temptation to at first trust fear and to doubt love.

Yet, there was a second biblical evidence suggesting to my own mind that Jesus, being fully human as we are, was caught up in a conflict between his own bodily fear and his own spiritual love. It happened, reportedly, on the night before his death by crucifixion.

Leading up to his crucifixion, Jesus reportedly experienced physically the sound of loud hosannas, the sight of a barren fruit tree and, perhaps not unrelated, the sight of money changers in the temple, among other events. Having wept earlier over Jerusalem and still earlier over the passing of friend, Lazarus, the last thing Jesus needed to see was his disciple, Judas, then walking out of the room at the mention of his impending betrayal. As if to identify fully with our own humanity, Jesus experienced fear of a painful death in ways that stirred a body to mind conversation not unlike our own if facing similar circumstances. Who can forget his garden of Gethsemane prayer, "*Abba, Father! All things are possible for You. Take this cup away from Me.*" -- Mark 14:36? Though using other wording, we've all probably experienced some type of self-talk in times of stress, and known something of a desperate body to mind conversation within ourselves. Who of us have not wrestled within ourselves over fearful uncertainties that were facing us?

But for Jesus, this particular uncertainty represented fear's heaviest stone within his own earthly lifetime. And for Jesus, fear meant the same two things I believe it means to all the rest of us. First, there is a desire to avoid whatever it is that is being feared. And secondly, there is a firm appeal for the mind to take control in a way that would end the chaos of impending uncertainty.

The way I'm viewing this body to mind appeal is that God, the Father, may have experienced in such moments an *ahab* type of love for his Son that became over-ruled by his *hesed* type of love for all humankind. The latter and most enduring love is what brought about a *naham* change of mind that decided not to take this cup from Jesus, the Son. In this way, the world's fear narrative for Jesus gave way to God's heavenly love narrative. I believe it was this decision by the parental mind of God Jesus called Father, that set in motion the very power of love's resurrection to roll away his own fear's heaviest stone.

To summarize before moving on within the story of my 3rd Great Awakening, I now believe God's very *essence* (the What) is spiritual and God's very *existence* (the Who) is mental and physical. *Essence*: The Holy Spirit or indwelling soul. *Existence*: The Father and Son as host temple for the Holy Spirit. God is love, and God is also lover.

You will find in what you have just read a rather heavy dose of God-talk that may seem altogether confusing at worst and altogether new at best. Or even altogether heretical in appearance. You may reason very differently concerning the scriptures. Together we may concede my own reasoning is grounded in my private experience rather than communal tradition.

No worries. At least on my own part, though you are entirely free to do so at will. My faith in love's dominant God story is based on my own understanding of scripture alongside the experience I call my 3rd Great Awakening. To understand my most recent awakening into love's dominant narrative for my own life, I will now take you to my next chapter on Sin. Perhaps there it will be clear what I consider to be the critical difference between ourselves and Jesus, sin and salvation, being 1/3 divine and 2/3 divine, being fear dominant and being love dominant.

Spoiler alert: it's all in the mind.

CHAPTER NINE

Sin

"Sin was a word once in everyone's mind, but is now rarely if ever heard. Does that mean that no sin is involved in all our troubles? Has no one committed sin? Where, indeed, did sin go? What became of it?" -- Karl Menninger, M.D.

Years ago, I taught an adult Sunday School class at our local church. During the summer months, when folks would be out of town or at least out of class more frequently, I typically dispensed with any other curriculum and offered up a 3-month series on "Christ and the Andy Griffith Show." I'd begin each class period with a video of one of those old Andy Griffin TV sitcoms from back in the 60's or thereabouts. Without commercials each episode would come in at around 20, leaving us time for some healthy discussion afterward. To make it easy on all concerned, especially myself as teacher, I would ask essentially two questions for our group discussion. First, "how are we maybe like Barney Fife was in this episode?" After sufficient sharing about one's own peculiarities, or those of one's spouse if he or she were somehow absent from class that day, we'd move on to the second question: "And how is Jesus Christ maybe like Sheriff Taylor was in this show?"

If you're never owned a television and are not familiar with this old iconic sitcom, the character of Barney Fife involved a small town Sheriff's deputy who was more than a bit undersized and sometimes afraid of his own shadow, and whose fears always put him in mind to seize power and take control. Whether it was arresting jaywalkers or lecturing children on the finer points of law enforcement, Deputy Fife had to take control in order to compensate for his own fears and insecurities in life. Barney Fife liked to hide behind the authority of his own badge, as when he would close the doors on one of the two town jail cells behind a newly alleged outlaw removed from those tough streets of Mayberry. His pattern of "inmate orientation" went something like this: Now here at the Rock, we have two basic rules. The first rule is: OBEY ALL THE RULES.

Meanwhile, the character of Andy Taylor involved the local

town Sheriff. Barney's boss. The guy who, unlike his ranting Deputy, spoke rather calmly and felt no need to wear any sidearm pistol to assert control over others. He read no one any riot acts, contrary to Barney Fife. It wasn't that Sheriff Taylor was fearless, mind you, but he just went about his duties in law enforcement by placing his faith in love somewhere above his faith in fear.   Such a plot was always lost on Deputy Fife, who appeared week after week as most faithful to his own life's fear story and more than a bit doubtful when it came to Sheriff Taylor's preferred love story.

I still find myself to this day thinking about old Barney Fife every time I go to confront one of my own sins. And I still question, do I have more faith in Christ's loving ways than Barney had in Andy's way of doing things?   Sometimes I'm like Barney, and I question God's way as being kind of, well, naïve about our tough streets. I may even doubt that God's love will do more than just make our bad situation worse. At such points, I'd make a really good Deputy Fife.

Week in and week out, year after year, I find myself tempted by the things going on in this world to make fear my aim instead of love.   I read or watch or hear the world's "breaking news" and next thing you know my body's at work trying to convince my mind that I have to do something about it all immediately.   Maybe it's that I have to tell someone else, post some dire warning on Facebook, or else I have to convince everyone around me that the sky is falling if we don't do this or that "asap." I'm more like Barney Fife than I'd like to admit.   All too often in these times, I find it easier to trust in my fears than in God's love, more like Mayberry's rattled deputy than I am their calm sheriff.

Now don't get me wrong. My bodily senses and emotions that inform my mind aren't necessary wrong, or right. They record the data and pass it on immediately so the mind can decide how best to respond. After which my mind does one of two things.   It either obeys my body and does one of those Barney Fife "Ready, Fire, Aim" maneuvers.   Or it stops to instead listen to what God may have to say about it all before I go off half-cocked and do or say something foolish.

Sin for me is like a default position of the mind. A position that always first says yes to the body and no to the soul whenever they are giving conflicted stories, or conflicted information for the mind's decision-making. Now there are plenty of times that my bodily senses reflect the world's message of truth. The problem of sin only comes about when those same senses instead reflect the world's lies or half-truths.

My sin comes not from my bodily sensations, which have no ability to discern truth from lies, but from my mental choices that, given a conflict between the world's information passed through my body and heaven's information passed through my soul, judge the latter as doubtful and the former as if somehow more trustworthy. Even though this happens quite instantly and unconsciously, my mind is the actual sinner within me. When my own mind resolves my internal conflicts by faithfully believing the world's lies passed along through my sensual bodily rather than heaven's truths passed along through my spiritual soul, I have taken step one in the process of sinning. My mind is acting on what is all too often the world's faulty information. And that action involves taking control at the expense of my better influence. Sinning, then, becomes my mind's choice to live out my fear story rather than God's preferred love story for my life. My sin starts with believing the world's occasional "fake news" as if it were fact.

Back in the early days around the time of my 1st Great Awakening, I was pretty sure that all my sins were centered around my body's desires. Somehow if I failed to just say "no" to my own desires, I was guilty and ready for the fires of some eternal hell. Or so I then thought. Not a whole lot changed for me in that arena of my faith until around the more recent time of my 3rd Great Awakening.

Once again it was an application of that old Methodist standby of reasoning by use of scripture, tradition and experience that caught my attention enough to wake me up anew. It caught my attention when it came to my own sin. In terms of scripture, my new interpretation of those three temptations of Jesus in the wilderness (as noted in previous chapter) impressed me with how much more Jesus was tempted by fear than by desire.

If human fears in the area of unmet needs for survival, security, and status (social belonging) can teach us anything, it is that fear is our body's way of giving our mind only two choices to decide between: fight or flight. Either of which we may experience as desire. The desire for more stems from our fear of less. Our desire to gain control stems from our primary fear of loss. We desire pride because we fear shame. It is my fear, not my desire, that sets in motion my sinful patterns of thinking and behaving.

Now at this point, I can imagine some thoughts you may be having. Am I saying it is a sin to be afraid? Am I saying Jesus sinned because he was afraid? The answers are no and no.

Fear, as I look at it, is the body's involuntary reflex to our world's stressors or events beyond our own control. Fear is an emotion triggered by our brain's central nervous system. We see, hear or otherwise sense data produced by our world. This fear is not sinful, but it the source of our heaviest temptation for the mind. Only the mind can sin. Not the soul. And not the body except as the accomplice to carry out our mind's sinful decisions.

Jesus did not sin in the wilderness, although his fearful body sent forth every temptation. But the reason he did not sin is that his mind, which I call the Father, rightly discerned the key difference between heaven's truth passed through his soul and the world's lies passed through his body.

As a body obeys the mind, so Jesus did what the Father (also informed by the Holy Spirit), decided was truer, and better, than his body's own preferred fight or flight. This was a large part of how Jesus practiced bodily self-sacrifice. He knew the fear, and the temptation, he was feeling inside his own body. But he trusted his mind more than his own body to make the right, and better, decision in dealing with the world around him.

A critical point in my own most recent awakening where my understanding of sin is concerned involves the difference between control and influence. Some may suggest this is a difference without a distinction, but I don't believe that's true. May have in the past, but I don't now.

Whether at a conscious or unconscious level, the human mind knows the difference between its self-talk with the body and its self-talk with the soul. The body passes on our world's messages of fear in the form of shouts directed at the mind. These shouts aim at driving the mind to take control over whatever situation the body is experiencing in our world. Such self-talk from body to mind may use words like "I must" or "I need" or even "I have to.... or else I will suffer some awful fate." Fear demands control. Or else.

This is where I go back to that classic example of Deputy Fife shouting for Sherriff Taylor to take control. Write a citation. Lock 'em up.

Meanwhile, the human mind is also engaging in self-talk

with the soul, even at an unconscious level. (I would contend it is prayer that renders the unconscious then conscious in our minds.) The soul passes on heaven's messages of love in the form of whispers directed at the mind. Not shouts. Whispers. And rather than driving the mind to take control over some worldly situation, the soul is then drawing the mind to give influence within that worldly situation. Such self-talk from soul to mind may whisper such words as "I may" or "I could" or even "I want to." "I might be able to give influence and then......" triggers a love of life, where the body's shouts of "I must be able to take control or else......" triggers a fear of death. The mind hears both types of self-talk, but what the mind then believes and decides affects our later consequences. Self-fulfilling consequences.

I'm going to ask you in this very moment to imagine something.

Please imagine that you are involved in two very close relationships. You might imagine them as a couple of friends, both parents, or any other two people important to your life. And with whom you have frequent contact.

Now pretend in your mind that one of these persons is often bothered by your own little imperfections to the point that this person tries to control your behavior. Tries to speak for you, to think and decide for you, to basically control your life if only to correct your imperfections as if their own life depended on it.

And then imagine that other person in your life. This one refuses to take control over you, to speak for you, think or decide for you. Instead, this person prefers to offer some helpful points, trying to influence you to make your own best or at least better decisions. All so you can learn to live your own best life.

Could you picture them both? Could you notice how very different these two were? So now consider this: which of these two persons in your life would you believe loves you the most? The one anxious to control, correct and perfect you? Or the one offering only influence that might empower you in helping yourself?

I bring up such a pretend scenario to illustrate the way in which I find myself to be a sinner.   I am sometimes bothered by other peoples' imperfections to the point that I choose not to lovingly influence them to make better decisions for themselves, but instead to fearfully control and correct them and make them right and perfect in my own judgment.   These I call my primary sins of commission.

At other times, if more severely bothered by other peoples' imperfections, my idea of fearful control may be to avoid them and steer myself in some opposite direction to escape their presence. Or to at least rid myself of having to see and hear and think about them any further. These I call my secondary sins of omission.

Whether by commission or omission, my sins involve my own wrong choices in life. Choices that are based on lies rather than truth. Choices based on fear rather than love. Choices that seek to control others rather than influence them. Choices more in line with Deputy Fife's character in the old TV show. Choices that are quite opposite those Sherriff Taylor, and Jesus Christ, would make if his own mind were doing the deciding.

Not only do I sin against other people in this way, I believe I sin against God in the same way. God, you might ask? Yes, I sin against God when I judge that he has acted imperfectly and needs my correction, my controlling ways that make him change what he would decide or do on his own. Remember the way Barney Fife went about correcting Sheriff Taylor in those old sitcoms? Vehemently insisting that Andy's love not get in the way of enforcing the letter of Mayberry law!

Sin is its own statement of faith in fear and doubt in love. Faith in the lies of this world and doubt in the truth of heaven.

While in that first appointment out of seminary as a full-time Associate Pastor for Growth at Sulphur Grove Church, l enjoyed my work of organizing teams to provide random acts of kindness throughout our community, as well as teams of hospitality servants when newcomers would arrive for worship, *Alpha* classes, and the like. But if my soul was content to continue doing this on into the future, my body was afraid I was wasting my skills and not helping enough people and, frankly, aging out of opportunities to really make the difference I'd expected to make in parish ministry. The local church to which I was appointed was encountering some financial difficulties due to a major building project, so I took that opportunity to ask for a lead pastor position elsewhere after only 3 years.

Remember the episode when Barney Fife decided it was time to move on from Mayberry and advance his career in the big city of Raleigh? Well, even if you don't, I do. And I did my next imitation of Barney in my own real life.

It went like this.

As I neared the age of 59, I experienced my very first appointment to be sole pastor at an aging congregation in a declining neighborhood of a nearby town. At Lagonda Church, I would essentially cut my preaching teeth and learn the administrative work of independently managing a small branch office of a large institution, to reference a business model. This is where my body and soul collided in serious conflict over the question of my fitness for pastoral ministry. It is also where I discovered what a sinner I was as a pastor.

Turning 60 that next year myself, I can remember feeling this great sense of fear that I was still failing to make any real difference in the world. Our very traditional church had failed to grow. Our funerals exceeded our baptisms. Our outreach ministry was small and, frankly, most of our neighbors didn't stop by or ever call except to request financial assistance with household emergencies. Our best success was in supplying the practical needs of many children in an elementary school with which we partnered. We also had some hard working volunteers who managed a weekly open gym for the youth of our neighborhood. Later, we became a successful host location for some weekly Narcotics Anonymous meetings. And our worship did come alive with some wonderful talents volunteering for liturgical dance, forming a team of about 15 individuals of all ages and races. Financially, we were catching up on what our denomination calls Conference or connectional apportionments. As a whole, we had a very active core of some 20 strong people carrying on laity work they had done over many years and using the same past methods. Methodists are rarely at ease with changing their methods.

Yet, my aims were in retrospect all about changing others' methods. The imperfections of that congregation began to bother me. And I began to see my work as pastor more in the arena of fearful control than of loving influence. In the years from 2005-2010, my mind would tell you that my body was constantly afraid our aging church was dying and that "I had to take control over the situation or else." Yet, the more I attempted to control the local church, its people and its surrounding neighborhood, the worse things actually became. I found myself working out of a fear narrative rather than living into God's preferred love story for our church.

Part of my own efforts to save the church included cutting my own salary package in half in 2009 by retiring from itinerant ministry since I was then age 62 and with benefit of full vesting and full ordination. This would enable us to stop the drain on our required health insurance premiums that were skyrocketing due to our small and aging beneficiary pool of Conference pastors. I would cut my hours and engage in some part-time clinical work contracting for mental health counseling at some area nursing homes. I would cover my own much cheaper health insurance on the open market using a Health Savings Account we had in our Conference credit union. Then I worked at controlling our aging building's capital repairs budget. Count this a major pipe dream, since our large building reflected the many home-made qualities found in many church buildings of yesteryear when codes were relaxed and laymen provided cheap labor. My somewhat smaller dream was for our congregation to actually pay our full share of District and Conference apportionments. And all this despite our nation's own economic "great recession" that was then in full bloom. I wasn't asking for much, right?

But then the roof fell in.

Well, not literally. Or at least not quite. Here is how that story unfolds.

It seemed that when not catching bats flying through our rather large 3-story building, we were soon to catch a raccoon. And then another. And another. Trap and release. Trap and release. Trap and release even further into the countryside. Our trustees did everything possible to break that chain migration. A tree was cut back that had a limb extending above our northern-most roof section. Tree looked nice, but no change where the raccoons were concerned. Except to now remove the exit should they otherwise decide to leave our building on their own.

More traps and releases. Aaargh!

In due time, a team of trustees and one of their Engineer brother-in-laws surveyed the space above the sanctuary itself and below the roof. These pesky raccoons had to be hunkered down in some "family room" of their own design. Somewhere. There, among the highest rafters, by way of unintended discovery, one of the heavy wooden beams supporting our roof was found severely fractured and ready to split apart and fall through our sanctuary's cathedral ceiling. That discovery nearly made a sinner out of all of us, but I was by far the chief of Lagonda sinners. I was afraid not only for our safety, but for our survival if we could not financially afford the needed repairs. And there was nothing I could do to control the situation short of relocating our worship services to another part of the building for safety's sake.

Thankfully, our voluntary Engineer brother-in-law and his team of trustees very capably built some trusses in support of that fractured beam and much money was again saved in the process. It was all a huge answer to prayer, but in the course of that crisis I learned something about my own fear. I had within my own body a fear of personal failure that spoke its own self-talk into my own mind, demanding that I take more and more control over our outside circumstances as a local church.

Instead, all that was needed was the loving influence of a group of volunteer raccoons, discovered by the even more loving influence of our volunteer trustees, and that Engineer brother-in-law who never sent us a bill. Without all of them we would never have located that fractured beam threatening to fall through our sanctuary ceiling.

My own fearful, sinful, control as pastor contributed nothing to the mix.

As time went on, several more situational changes triggered my fearful temptation to take control. While chairing a clergy cluster among my colleagues in ministry for my denomination within our city, we focused our attention on the prospect of a 7-church merger or partnership that would create a new and larger congregation with a vision that would include a new 21st century building in a new location. After much time and energy was expended, much of our vision was lost. Especially, the part involving a multi-racial and multi-cultural critical mass of people across the age and class spectrum. We were left with only three mostly aging, mostly Caucasian, parishes willing to participate, ours being one of them. All three shared a common demography. So much for our vision of diversity. Within the next year, this new partnership had completed itself to the best of everyone's ability and a new pastor was appointed to lead the new 3-in-1 congregation into its future. I would serve an interim appointment at a different congregation out of town, then work without appointment for a few more years in part-time ministry back with Sulphur Grove Church where my pastoral career began.

Throughout this time period, I made a clarifying discovery about myself. In times of greatest uncertainty, when the world around me is spinning with change, I clearly experience a shift in my own faith paradigm. I become doubtful that love is enough. Doubtful that influence can possibly be as powerful as outright control. Doubtful that love will endure forever, or will never end. I become faithful instead to my own fears as fed by the world's bad news. I begin to fear my own failure, and I make decisions aimed at controlling the very world I'm called to instead influence

Amidst my 3rd Great Awakening, this is where my own sin is most evident. Instead of following the Christ of Calvary who surrendered all control over others, even inviting us to do the same while taking up our own crosses, my own mind has too often chosen the path of fearful control over a world of others who's like imperfections I fail to accept. My mind has sinfully chosen to follow after my body's demands and not to follow the Jesus of my soul's desire and advice.

Whenever I have sinfully chosen to privilege the body that drives me to fearfully seek control over the "other," these five unintended consequences seem to occur:
1. I lose my loving influence in relation to others. That's right, the more control I seek to gain in my relationships, the more influence I end up losing.
2. The more control I seek, the more inclined I am to blame and even scapegoat those who most powerfully resist my control.
3. The more I live out of my fear story, the more separated I am from God who, when faced with that same human fear story, chose instead to live into his own love story in this world.
4. And the more I seek after a controlling god in whom I fear, the farther I am from finding the influential God who casts out all fear in favor of love.
5. My pastoral fear story becomes the self-fulfilling prophecy of failure.

Hell, I have come to believe, is the consequence caused by my own sinful choices. It is a phenomenon of this world, whose kingdoms of fearful control seek to over-rule God's Kingdom of loving influence. When my bodily kingdom seeks to over-rule my soul's spiritual Kingdom, my mind's choice to appease my body brings about my own hellish consequences. Such sinful decisions then place my soul in the position of outside intruder, invading my body's own space as some foreign competitor. Likening this to our body's own physical immune system, it is as if sin is then my mind's auto-immune disease in relation to my soul.

Here is how such a spiritual auto-immune disease takes hold. Instead of using my spiritual antibodies to attack the foreign and faulty information my mind receives from the world through my body, it is as if my mind attacks the soul as a perceived foreign object that does not belong inside my body. Triangulated between my control-driven body and my influence-drawn soul, my mind sides with my body in order to cast out God's heavenly love. My mind's auto-immune response to my soul works to externalize the very part of me that could help to heal my disease.

Sin is rooted in my mind's own faulty decision-making system that rewards my body's lies and resists the soul's truths. And when my sin results, and my hellish consequence occurs, it is always because my mind wrongfully chose to say yes to my body's lies by default and no to my soul's truth as if it were a foreign object that didn't belong. Again, this makes my personal sins of commission and omission into symptoms of what I now am calling my spiritual auto-immune disorder (SAD).

I wonder if this is not close to what the apostle Paul was considering when he wrote about his own sin in Romans 7: "*I do not understand my own actions. For I do not do what I want, but I do the very thing I hate. Now if I do what I do not want, I agree that the law is good. But in fact it is no longer I that do it, but sin that dwells within me" (Romans 7:15-17).*

At the very least this scripture from our New Testament suggests that Paul was aware of a conflict within his own mind. He seemed to know he was making bad choices because the Jewish Law had proven this to him. Yet, he could not see a way of healing himself from such a spiritual auto-immune disease. The lies coming to mind through his own body were attacking God's truth coming in through his soul. He writes, *"So I find this law at work: Although I want to do good, evil is right there with me. For in my inner being I delight in God's law; but I see another law at work in me, waging war against the law of my mind and making me a prisoner of the law of sin at work within me" (Romans 7:21-23).* Paul seemed to know his mind's bad decisions were being strongly affected by these opposing sources of information, his body's fearful control seeming to reject the soul's loving influence before he could rightly act upon it. For Paul the fearful control that triggered his becoming *"chief among sinners"* (I Timothy 1:15) happened when, as Saul, his fear of those Jews who followed Christ caused him to seek control over them pursuant to their own death.

This same Biblical writer then arrives at the point of asking and answering a question for our own further consideration. Having to do with the matter of his own sins, he writes: *"Wretched man that I am! Who will rescue me from this body of death? Thanks be to God, who delivers me through Jesus Christ our Lord"* (Romans 7:24-25).

CHAPTER TEN

Salvation

"For God so loved the world that he gave his only Son, so that everyone who believes in him may not perish but may have eternal life" -- John 3:16

"We know love by this, that he laid down his life for us—and we ought to lay down our lives for one another" -- 1 John 3:16

"When Christ calls a man, he bids him come and die." -- Deitrich Bonhoeffer

Many years ago I liked to attend my all-time favorite training center for continued professional education units, the Cape Cod Summer Institute. Each morning would be four hours of intensive training followed by an afternoon on the beach for doing whatever other adventures I wanted. I would take my wife along. We had some great times, and we considered this the high point of our annual summer vacation.

One year the course I signed up for was on Hypnotherapy, conducted by one of the late Dr. Milton Erickson's protégés named William O'Hanlon. As with most one-week intensives, such a course offered a fairly strong body of knowledge but very little in way of practical skill-building opportunities. But to expand whatever skill set we each brought to the training, O'Hanlon encouraged our application of these therapeutic theories. We were to practice using hypnotherapy with some "willing participant" (to be found in or out of the conference room) at a time of his or her own choosing during the afternoon or evening hours.

My wife volunteered to be my first ever "willing participant." At least I think she volunteered.

We made our way to a secluded, pristine sandy beach along the Cape Cod National Seashore. We found a flat space to spread our blanket. We soaked up some rays and shared some relaxing conversation together. And after a while I ventured into some words I thought might offer her at least a speck of healing in the area of "low self-esteem" she identified as a problem she would like to better gain some power over in her own life.

To say that I was the world's most awkward hypnotherapist in those moments would be perhaps the slightest of exaggerations. I recall our practice session being something of a guided meditation with some early attention to the senses of sight, sound, touch, and smell in particular. After all, we were sitting in the summer sunshine, warm to the touch, on soft fine sand cushioned by our comfy blanket, the salty scent of ocean air stirred by a gentle breeze, the sound of an ocean tide washing ashore, in, out, in, out in a perfect hypnotic rhythm rivaled only by the rhythm of our own internal organs, the heart beating and the lungs breathing, in, out, in, out.

As I stumbled along in my own words of possible relaxation and even trance induction, I noticed something rather interesting. I was very nearly falling asleep myself. I was ready to lie back onto the blanket myself for a nice afternoon nap on that warm, breezy summer day. As I mouthed words to the effect that, closing our eyes and noticing only the inner workings of our own healthy hearts and lungs, we both began to forget the outer sights and sounds and sensations of the world around us. We both learned to ignore every outside distraction except the sound of my voice. Forgetting the noise of this world's own hurts and sometimes insults and misunderstandings, we were both free to pay attention to the healing powers within ourselves. Healing that could re-mind us of our great worth as persons, our higher self-esteem, and our own strengths and abilities the outside world may not even know we have.

After a while, I seemed to tire of this internal journey to that stronger place inside and Sue and I both opened our eyes as if re-awakened from a rather vague but beautiful dream we could only partially recall. To this day, I can't say whether this little practice session amidst that idyllic and most hypnotic of venues lasted 5 minutes or an hour. It was probably somewhere in between. Neither of us were cured, but we were both equally relaxed by the end of "practice."

My point in sharing this is two-fold.

First, I wonder if there is not something of a "low self-esteem" problem in all of us because of sin. Our sin is actually the "fear story" we receive from our body's inevitable attention to the world's outer stimuli. Make that negative stimuli, for effect. Shouts of "fearful control" distracting us from the internal wisdom, and the "preferred love story" of our own souls. God's Spirit is still beating in rhythm above our noisy world, but the worldly fears are like the roar of an ocean at times drowning out the still small voice of the Master within us. Fear drives us to attend to the outer stimuli rather than the quiet sound of our own internal heartbeats. Yet it is those very heartbeats within that sustain our lives, not the roar of any distracting ocean tides beyond. The body's attention to this loudest sound around seems to attack the soul's loving whispers within. Such an attack is what in the previous chapter I labeled as a spiritual auto-immune disease, the body convincing the mind to attack the soul that would otherwise heal it of some internalized fear problem. Such a problem as "low self-esteem."

One of my favorite Psalms of David begins with these words: *"God is our refuge and strength, a very present help in trouble. Therefore, we will not fear, though the earth should change, though the mountains shake in the heart of the sea; though its waters roar and foam."* David goes on to end that same 46th Psalm with: *"Be still, and know that I am God! I am exalted over the nations; I am exalted in the earth. The LORD of hosts is with us; the God of Jacob is our refuge."*

In a parallel theme, David writes, *"The LORD is my light and my salvation; whom shall I fear? The LORD is the stronghold of my life; of whom shall I be afraid?"* -- Psalm 27:1.

My second reason for sharing the hypnosis story is that, as I found myself so sleepily identified with my wife amidst my trance induced suggestion for relief from her own low self-esteem, I now believe God enters into salvation "with" us rather than "for" us. Just as I essentially hypnotized myself along with my wife, I wonder if Jesus, the Christ, did not join in our own therapeutic work upon the cross, strange as that at first sounds. Upon the cross, perhaps God was able through the body of Jesus to understand what it was like for us to be misunderstood by other people, abused by some and neglected by others, wrongly condemned into a position of lowly esteem. God was able to join in our suffering and in our healing perhaps like I joined with my wife that day on the sandy banks of Cape Cod. To our own "low self-esteem" problem, God could now say "been there, done that, know how that feels." On the cross of Calvary.

Stemming from my own 3rd Great Awakening, I came to have a very different understanding of how it is God saves us from our sins through Jesus Christ. But before explaining that new understanding, let me first account for my previous understandings and how these came to be.

Backing up to my 1st Awakening as shared earlier, I first came to understand myself as a sinner bound for an external Hell of eternal conscious torment should I fail to accept Jesus as having died to pay the penalty for my sin. My salvation depended on my praying the right words of "I'm sorry for all of my many sins, thank you for sending Jesus to die for me on the cross, and please save me from going to hell for my own sins when I die."

Prior to any seminary studies, I had no real understanding of where my own belief in that old rugged cross really originated. I had supposed it was the one and only biblical Gospel. And that it came from Christ himself. I assumed that somewhere in all the New Testament, Jesus had declared that he would really die so those who believed in him as their personal Savior could go to heaven when they died.

Little did I know that Jesus never said any such thing. Not even close!

Most of my Bible training up to that point had been a series of memorized individual verses scattered about the scriptures. I knew the Bible stories from my youth, but I had no "holistic" understanding of the "holy" Biblical story. My parents did a wonderful job of reading the Bible to me, one passage or story at a time. They gifted me with Bibles growing up, and I still have them all including a Living Bible from back in 1971, green cover and all. Cover is badly worn, pages are loose here and there, but it turned into my favorite Bible for years to come. Still, my years of exposure to church attendance 2-3 times weekly, Vacation Bible School, Youth Fellowship, Youth for Christ, and, of course, summer "church camp," gave me lots of bricks but no mortar in between to hold it all together. I accepted John 3:3 and 3:16 for my salvation, but these were simply two bricks stacked atop each other (easily knocked down) when I approached my college years and later seminary years beginning in 1968. I took these two verses by Jesus as somehow suggesting that if I said the sinner's prayer with adequate conviction, I would be born again and eligible for a heavenly salvation from my sin upon my death here on earth.

Other scriptural proof-texting then added to my understanding of such salvation. In the main, these verses flow pretty much as follows:

- Isaiah 53:4-6, 10, 11—"Surely he has borne our griefs and carried our sorrows; yet we esteemed him stricken, smitten by God, and afflicted. But he was wounded for our transgressions, he was bruised for our iniquities; upon him was the chastisement that made us whole, and with his stripes we are healed. All we like sheep have gone astray; we have turned everyone to his own way; and the LORD has laid on him the iniquity of us all ... It was the will of the LORD to bruise him; he has put him to grief; when he makes himself an offering for sin ... By his knowledge shall the righteous one, my servant, make many to be accounted righteous; and he shall bear their iniquities."

- Romans 3:23-26—"All have sinned and fall short of the glory of God; they are now justified by his grace as a gift, through the redemption that is in Christ Jesus, whom God put forward as a sacrifice of atonement by his blood, effective through faith. He did this to show his righteousness, because in his divine forbearance he had passed over the sins previously committed; it was to prove at the present time that he himself is righteous and that he justifies the one who has faith in Jesus."

- 2 Corinthians 5:21—"For our sake he made him to be sin who knew no sin, so that in him we might become the righteousness of God."

- Galatians 3:10, 13—"All who rely on works of the law are under a curse; for it is written, 'Cursed be everyone who does not abide by all things written in the book of the law, and do them.' ... Christ redeemed us from the curse of the law, having become a curse for us - for it is written, 'Cursed be everyone who hangs on a tree.'"

- 1 Peter 2:24—"He himself bore our sins in his body on the tree, that we might die to sin and live to righteousness."

- 1 Peter 3:18—"For Christ also died for sins once for all, the righteous for the unrighteous, that he might bring us to God."

All of these informed my understanding of scriptural salvation at the point of my 1st Great Awakening leading up to my arrival at seminary in 1968. My faith in this particular love story of divine salvation evolved out of a rather exhausted fear story underlying my own low self-esteem. What I then lacked was any real understanding of where in the world that fear story itself was coming from.

This may be a good time to also backtrack a ways on how I then understood sin in my life. As noted in the previous chapter, I've more recently come to understand sin as our human mind's decision to live out a fear story to achieve our own "mighty control" instead of God's love story that subjects us to having only a "mere influence." My own such decision to sin involves trusting in control rather than influence, fear rather than love, my body rather than my soul, and trusting the opposing messages of own body instead of God's own body (Jesus Christ). Again, I now view sin as a spiritual autoimmune disease where my body's lies attack the very antidote of my soul's truth; the truth embodied and fully revealed in Jesus of Nazareth.

Which is a long, long ways from how I used to view sin as leading up to my need for salvation.

I had grown up thinking that sin was instead a decision to disobey God's angry commands. A decision to resist God's shouts of control over me. Any single disobedience would separate me from God's perfection and place me under God's controlling wrath and judgment. Jesus, I had learned in my youth, was united with God's perfection and so he loved me enough to die for me on the cross, accepting God's wrath and judgment in my place. At the point of my 1st Awakening, I had no name for such a thought about sin and salvation. I simply called it "Christianity."

Starting in 1968, that 1st Awakening to what I then understood as God's love for me through Christ's death on the cross to keep me out of hell was beginning to unravel. That understanding of salvation, of atonement with God and of love itself, would come to have a name upon my first entry into seminary. That name would be *Penal Substitution*.

Charles Hodge was a 19th century theologian and Princeton Seminary professor who ascribed to the Calvinist Reformed wing of Protestant Christianity. He taught a particular understanding of salvation called *Penal Substitution* that he traced to John Calvin with earlier contributions from Anselm of Canterbury and later on Martin Luther. This is the view that God is demanding of eternal punishment for those who have sinned and only the perfect Christ could satisfy God's wrath against humanity's sin, thus requiring his death upon the cross as penalty for our personal sins.

My early seminary work helped me gain added perspective in such matters through the study of church history as well as biblical theology. Such a perspective started me on the long pathway of searching out alternatives to this theory of salvation and atonement, especially if other theories were grounded in actual biblical theology and earlier church history (say, prior to Anselm's arrival roughly a thousand years after the biblical Acts of the Apostles).

By the time of my later seminary work and my 2nd Great Awakening, I had fairly well settled upon a theory of salvation originating with Origen (pardon the pun), a 2nd century Egyptian Christian theologian who made strong work out of this quote from Jesus found in Mark 10:45 and Matthew 20:28, *"For the Son of Man came not to be served but to serve, and to give his life a ransom for many."*

This work of Origen came to be called the *Ransom* theory of salvation forming the basis for what Augustine later developed as the *Christus Victor* theory, believing that Christ's death on the cross was not to satisfy or appease God, but rather Satan. Jesus thus served God's most brilliant plot to destroy Satan's power at the point of his own resurrection.

Upon resuming my seminary work, I recall at one point writing a paper not long after the 9/11 terrorist attack that I chose to entitle, "The Terrorism of Satan." There I hypothesized that the devil acted to essentially kidnap God's human creation and hold his children all for ransom under threat of death. God made a deal to send his own son to earth as an act of "exchanged ransom" if the devil would release all the children. The devil finally came to accept the deal but only after convincing the children they would need to first kill this man named Jesus. Otherwise, they would incur God's angry wrath for not doing so. (Note the story of Caiaphas within the biblical crucifixion story.) God's children believed that lie by the devil and did kill Jesus. Afterward, some believed another lie stating they would, having now made God even more enraged than before, be better off staying with the devil in the only safe home they'd ever known. Others doubted that lie and, believing the death of Jesus really had paid their ransom, did escape according to Satan's deal with God and were finally free from the hell they had been born into.

So went my own retelling of the salvation story that, unlike the *Penal Substitution* theory of my childhood, was based on something Jesus actually did say according to our scriptures.

My 2nd Awakening faith in God's loving plan for salvation, based on the Ransom theory that Origen first conceived some 1700 years prior to Charles Hodge's modernized Penal *Substitution* theory, was in retrospect a most definite upgrade. Don't ask me how Hodge's unbiblical theory could pass muster with biblical fundamentalist theologians even today. I considered Origen's and Augustine's theology far more scriptural than Anselm's and Calvin's, which had no connection with the "vine" of Christ's own teachings.

In any case, the seeds for my 3rd Awakening faith in God's loving plan for salvation were planted sometime after completing my seminary degree in 2002. There were two different post-seminary factors then stirring my own doubts about even Origin's 2nd century *Ransom* theory of salvation.

The first of these factors was a post-modern anthropologist named Rene Girard, a French Christian who offered up a very new twist on the old *Ransom* and *Christus Victor* theories of salvation. His own *Mimetic* theory began with a very new definition of sin as being *mimetic rivalry*, which produces a problem in our lives that then seeks out a scapegoating solution. Such a problem, in my understanding of Girard's theory, centered around our primary sin of coveting our neighbor.

As best I could understand Girard back in seminary (2000-2002), his foundational belief was that all human desire is mimetic (i.e., we borrow our desires from other people within our immediate culture). Sin originates when our borrowed (or coveted) desires bring us into interpersonal conflict and rivalry. Evil itself is found in the use of scapegoating (sacrificing of the other) to resolve our conflict and rivalry. Girard believed that the scapegoat mechanism was the origin of sacrifice and the foundation of human culture. He also believed that religion was necessary in human culture to control the violence that came from the sins of *mimetic rivalry*. Where Christ and even the Christian religion are concerned, his death by scapegoating on the cross scandalizes our human sins and forces us to repent of our own sins and violence against our own rivals. By repentance and turning away from such sinful coveting or desire, such conflict, and such scapegoating we are saved.

What interested me most in this theory of sin and salvation contributed by Rene Girard was its success in undoing the evils of

Caiaphas, Jerusalem's High Priest, who said, *"You do not realize that it is better for you that one man die for the people than that the whole nation perish"* --John 11:50. Our scandal is in having agreed with Caiaphas in viewing Jesus as our "better him than us" substitute. In effect, the theory of *Penal Substitution* is itself scandalized, as is any other theory that scapegoats Jesus by having him die so we, like the biblical Caiaphas, can go on living. To be sure, Girard seemed most reasonable to me in placing Christ on the cross not "for" our sins so we could go free, but rather "from" our sins so we could feel and repent of our own guilt.

There was a second factor taken away from seminary that stirred further doubt and pointed me further in the direction of my next Awakening. It had to do with my improved understanding of the ancient cultures in which the original biblical writers and readers were actually situated long before Christ's crucifixion. To gain a more reasoned understanding of scriptural authority, I learned the importance of knowing the when and where and why behind the "what" of scriptural content. In other words, I learned to better understand the intent behind the content when reading the Bible.

For example, consider the Biblical content having to do with this entire notion of God's demand for sacrifice to achieve salvation or atonement. We get a rather early idea from Genesis 4 about how it is God views plant (grain) or animal (blood) sacrifice when we read of Cain and Abel. And we go on to read of how our sacrifices meet God's requirements for appeasement, forgiveness, salvation or atonement per Genesis 8 and later 15, or Exodus 20, or Leviticus 8 or Numbers 18 or Deuteronomy 12. Plenty of support is found biblically for the whole theory of salvation by means of sacrificial offerings before God.

Only to turn around and read other Bible passages such as these: *"For thou desirest not sacrifice ... thou delightest not in burnt offerings."* --Psalm 51:16(KJV). And then these words from the prophets upon speaking for God: *"I delight not in the blood of bulls, or of lambs, or of he goats"* -- Isaiah 1:11; *"He that killeth an ox is as if he slew a man"*--Isaiah 66:3(KJV); *"Your burnt offerings are not acceptable, nor your sacrifices sweet unto me"* --Jeremiah 6:20; *"for I spoke _not_ unto your fathers, nor commanded them in the day that I brought them out of the land of Egypt, concerning burnt offerings or sacrifices"*--Jeremiah 7:21-22; *"For I desired mercy, and not sacrifice; and the knowledge of God more than burnt offerings"*--Hosea 6:6; *"with what shall I come before the* LORD *and bow down before the exalted God? Shall I come before him with burnt offerings, with calves a year old. Will the* LORD *be pleased with thousands of rams, with ten thousand rivers of olive oil? Shall I offer my firstborn for my transgression, the fruit of my body for the sin of my soul? He has shown you, O mortal, what is good. And what does the* LORD *require of you? To act justly and to love mercy and to walk humbly with your God"* --Micah 6:6-8.

Jesus himself was reported by Matthew to confirm such prophetic messages from God when saying *"I will have mercy, and not sacrifice"*-- Matthew 9:13. and again, *"If you had known what these words mean, 'I desire mercy, not sacrifice,' you would not have condemned the innocent"* --Matthew 12:7.

So now what?

Does God require a blood sacrifice such as was performed by Jesus at the cross of crucifixion? Or not? If not, is there any other plan of salvation to be found in the Bible?

I began to notice that the intent behind scriptural content began not with the persons of Moses or Abraham, but rather the respective cultures in which they were each nurtured. Biblical anthropologists such as Alice Linsley and Biblical archeologists such as William Hallo influenced my understanding in new ways that would point me away from any salvation theories as related to blood or other burnt sacrifices.

Pre-biblical writings and artifacts depict cultures both in ancient Mesopotamia, home to Abraham in his formative years, and in ancient Egypt, home to Moses in his formative years, involving sacrifices to the angry gods. Why were the gods angry? Per ancient cultures, when bad things happened in the world without scientific or other reasonable explanation, the cause was typically assumed to be the angry gods. Likewise, to bring an end to such bad things or keep them from happening again required some form of appeasement in relation to these angry gods. The Kushites of Ur in ancient Mesopotamia typically offered grain sacrifices to appease them. Their intent was to satisfy their gods' hunger as an assumed reason for their gods' angry behaviors. Hence, a grain offering would appease that hunger. Dr. Hallo has, per his own science, unearthed ancient pre-biblical altars from the land of Abraham's youth that suggest burnt sacrifices occurred long before Abraham ever received such an idea from Yahweh in the book of Genesis.

Where Abram (later Abraham) departed from his upbringing was to view God as one, not many. He could not unsee what he had seen as a boy involving burnt offerings at a sacrificial alter intent upon appeasing their god's anger born of hunger. And it was this intent that was brought to the content of Abraham's new monotheistic Hebrew culture in the land of Canaan.

Likewise, in Egypt, I came to understand that their appeasement of angry gods often took the form of animal sacrifice, where animal blood was burnt into ancient pre-biblical altars. Moses grew up with such religious rituals prior to discovering his Hebrew origins and joining the Abrahamic culture of his new identity.

Other anthropologists and archeologists may speak to such ancient religious rituals as child sacrifice, or other animal and plant sacrifices as are implicated in the biblical quarrel between Cain and Abel. From that story, you may recall the Mosaic culture won the day and gave the nod to Cain over Abel, for God preferred his animal (Moses's Egyptian) sacrifice to Abel's grain (Abraham's Mesopotamian) sacrifice. In any case, my own mind has faith that God's love for the ancient Hebrews would meet them where they were culturally in their first place. Only then would God be able to help influence them away from first child sacrifice, then burnt or blood offerings altogether. The biblical fear story wherein the angry God requires painful suffering for appeasement is, for my more recent understanding, truly a story of sin and not of salvation. The true salvation story would be revealed by Jesus. And it would be the ultimate love story.

Such studies and new understandings from my return to Dayton's United Theological Seminary led me in a direction well beyond my then *Ransom* theory of God's salvation. By the time of my 3rd Great Awakening a decade or so after graduation, I had developed my own mind's version of the *Moral Exemplar* theory first defined by the 2nd-century theologian, Irenaeus.
It was Irenaeus who taught that through God's transcendent love, Jesus Christ became what we are so we could become what he is. This "salvation by moral example," given church traditions that began with Irenaeus and continued a full millennium later with the work of Peter Abelard (1079-1142), situates God's mighty act of atonement at the cross of Christ where we are saved not by Christ but "with" Christ. We join in Christ's resurrection as we join "first"

in his crucifixion, taking up our own cross, sacrificing or losing our own lives. Indeed, our baptism with Christ is unto our own crucifixion and resurrection, not just our own resurrection. Paul put it this way in Romans 6:3, *"Do you not know that all of us who have been baptized into Christ Jesus are baptized into his death?"* In this *Moral Exemplar* understanding of salvation, Jesus in no way suffered and bled upon the sacrificial altar to appease God's anger and punishment, nor did he substitute for our death as a ransom unto Satan for our freedom. Rather, as Irenaeus would say, Jesus *"became what we are, that he might make us to be what he is."* We are atoned (at-oned) by dying "with" Jesus to our *bodily fear* ("be not afraid") and rising "with" Jesus to our *spiritual love* ("love never ends"). Jesus joined in our fearful crucifixion that we might join in his loving resurrection. This is God's sacramental work of grace in both our Baptism and Communion.

While many, perhaps even within United Seminary, may now deem me a heretic, I can only express here the full story of where my more recent 3rd Great Awakening has taken me. I remind myself more nowadays of Peter Abelard, who followed biblical authority as reasoned in his own mind using the traditions brought forth by Irenaeus and even Augustine later on. It is this tradition of Irenaeus up through Abelard that now helps me in reasoning the biblical authority of Jesus, who therein calls us to follow him carrying our own crosses of crucifixion as we lay down our own lives before being saved.

Of highest biblical authority, in my own mind, is the use of the Greek word *sozo* in connection with the sayings of Jesus in scripture. The word most literally means to save, to be saved, to be delivered, to be healed, to be in right relationship with God. And his most pointed use of this word in the biblical text came in these words found in all three synoptic Gospels: *"If any want to become my followers, let them deny themselves and take up their cross and follow me, for those who want to save (sozo) their life will lose it, and those who lose their life for my sake, and for the sake of the gospel, will save (sozo) it"* -- Matthew 16:25, Mark 8:35, Luke 9:24 and 17:33. Even the Gospel of John seems to concur by quoting Jesus as saying, *"unless a grain of wheat falls into the earth and dies, it remains just a single grain; but if it dies, it bears much fruit. Those who love their life lose it, and those who hate their life in this world will keep it for eternal life. Whoever serves me must follow me, and where I am, there will my servant be also."* -- John 12:24-26. The context in all four of these texts being Christ's own impending death as it applies to our *sozo* or being saved.

Jesus apparently believed rather strongly that the cross was not his alone to carry. Death was not his alone to suffer. Nor ours alone, for that matter. The cross is that common place where our human fears go to die.

Indeed, this conjoint cross of self-sacrifice was to be our sharing in the Kingdom, meaning we must all take up our cross and carry it "with" him. Such is the unique "salvation Gospel" (or *sozo* in the Greek) from Christ himself that appears in all four New Testament (Covenant) Gospels. Such is the unique "messianic prophecy" about Christ from Isaiah 7:14 that is said to be named or properly titled as Immanuel. The Hebrew words being *immanu* ("with us") and *el* ("God"). It was altogether in God's character to be "with" the people he was saving from slavery or from the battlefield. The significance throughout scripture of any successful outcome, salvation included, is that we cannot succeed without God's work and God will not succeed without our work. We're in this together. Hence, we are atoned "with" the crucified Christ when we follow his *moral exemplar*.

In a seldom told love-over-fear story, the great British hymnist, Thomas Shepherd, left the Anglican Priesthood to pastor Nottingham's independent, non-comformist Castle Hill Meeting House in 1694, after daring to write a controversial hymn one year earlier.1 Its words reflect what it is that I've finally come to understand about God's plan for our salvation. In some ways it summarizes the whole of my 3rd Great Awakening. The opening verse goes like this:

> *Must Jesus bear the cross alone,*
> *And all the world go free?*
> *No, there's a cross for everyone*
> *And there's a cross for me.*

When I survey the wondrous cross of Jesus, I often consider a concept from my years of clinical experience in working to heal the human symptoms of a depressed mood. In the field of mental health counseling, it is widely accepted that helping the depressed individual requires doing as much as possible "with" that person and little as possible "for" him or her.   Such a common axiom is often the first point of coaching in relation to the depressed person's family members.   For them, this is wildly counter-intuitive and goes against the grain of what they've long believed is true.   In the context of family counseling, folks may well drag their family member off to a different therapist who will tell them instead what to do "for" and not "with" their loved one.   Inwardly, they are seeking to be in control over the fear that they have somehow possibly failed their loved one.   Unknown even to themselves, they may seek control over their loved one's moods in ways quite counter-productive. A vicious cycle then traps both patient and family into dysfunction as they assume the impossible task of fighting these depressed moods "for" their loved one.

Therapists and Pastors alike would be much wealthier if paid a dollar for every time people complain that they have had to sacrificially "do for" someone in order to save him or her from self-neglect or self-destruction. We could all start, I suppose, with the spouse of nearly every alcoholic we've ever met.

Personally, I know of an alcoholic's spouse who chose, after failing at everything else, to drink right along "with" the alcoholic. Due to far lowered tolerance, the spouse became sickly drunk before the alcoholic even felt the first buzz of intoxication. This had the effect of motivating the alcoholic to then stay sober enough to at least take this staggering spouse home and properly attend to that pathetic drunk. It turned into something of a therapeutic role reversal.   And it worked until the alcoholic needed a more selfish reason to actually stay sober.   I thought it was an ingenious example of how doing "with" can produce "loving influence" truly more powerful than "fearful control" ever could.

If someone else is "out of control" over his or her own life, it is nearly universal that we will, by default, take over "for" them. We avoid doing much of anything "with" them. Quite often in the short run this is rather rewarding for us. The victim we seek to rescue is pleased by our rescue efforts and quite grateful the next morning. Or, if not, we sit in judgement over the "ingrate" who refused to thank us for having taken control of their out-of-control situation. That is a Christian martyrdom we often step into ourselves, despite Jesus having done no such thing "for" us per my current belief.

What I now wonder is this: what if Jesus didn't come to die for our sins after all?

What if blood sacrifice had nothing to do with our salvation? What if his death does nothing to atone or reconcile or restore our separated relationship with God? What if Jesus was not a martyr at all but rather a companion who is broken in communion "with" and not for us? What if he instead came to die with us? To die with us upon our communal cross for the sake of our at-one-ment? What if this is what the biblical *sozo* meant as Jesus explained his own death?

Is it possible that Jesus is only the lamb of God who is identified "with" us as sheep in facing our own fears, and only the good shepherd who then leads by example of how to rise again by means of love's resurrection? For me, at least, that is truly what makes Jesus the lamb fully human and Jesus the good shepherd fully divine. The lamb with whom we die and the shepherd with whom we rise.

To me it is no accident that Jesus was crucified "with" two other sinners. All four Gospels make this explicitly clear. He did not die alone. He died with others, likely one on either side of him. If, as some suggest, he died for the murderer, Barabbas, who then represents all of us, surely there is reason to think he died "with" us in relation to the alleged thieves at his side, who may represent us even more than Barabbas given that classic allegory.

This has become my new understanding of God's great love and amazing grace. Jesus saves a wretch like us by becoming a wretch "with" us. Broken. Bleeding. Wretched. Ridiculed. Misunderstood. Traumatized. Abused by some and neglected by others.

Dare I say "low self-esteem?"

Even in death Jesus is "with" us and like us. I now believe that Jesus comes to share our own cross. To be crucified with us. To live with us even in our heaviest of fears and uncertainties. To be reconciled with us, God's Body with ours, God's Mind with ours, God's Soul with ours. God's image in which we are all created now restored as "whole" and again holy.

Okay, if you're following me so far into my 3rd Great Awakening's faith in God's preferred love story "with" us, let us walk into some even taller weeds together involving biblical authority. You might want to brace yourself for this one.

A very early church tradition entered our Christian reasoning and experience that involved Paul's biblical letters. In these letters, he commonly uses the Greek word for grace, charis, as it applies to our salvation through Jesus Christ. Perhaps the classic verse in Protestant theology concerning biblical authority as applied to Christian salvation is this: *"For by grace (charis) you have been saved through faith, and this is not your own doing; it is the gift of God"* – Ephesians 2:8. We like to even sing of God's amazing grace and we've throughout Protestant traditions, at least, hung our hats upon the belief that God's grace (*charis*) saves us. We place our faith in that grace as rooted in Paul's own biblical theory of salvation.

Yet, there is more to biblical authority than what we call the apostolic epistles to the churches, pastors, etc. There is the teaching of Jesus as written after those epistles but appearing in front as the New Testament Gospels. There we read of Jesus proclaiming the good news of grace (*charis*) exactly, are you ready for this, zero times. Instead, Jesus spoke using one of three Greek words we translate in English as being love, *agape,* or its active tense, *agapao, in* roughly 40 different references. In what amounts to the only commandment Jesus ever gave us, we find these words: *"I give you a new commandment, that you love (agapao) one another. Just as I have loved (agapao) you, you also should love (agapao) one another"* -- John 13:34. Jesus taught his original disciples nothing at all about grace (*charis*) but absolutely everything there is to know about love (*agape*), the essence that becomes *(agapao)* in active existence.

To this most Christians might now say that grace and love are distinctions without a difference. In other words, what's my point?

My point is not that grace is in any way wrong for us to accept or place our faith in where God is concerned. Nor is it wrong for us to practice grace on behalf of others. I believe it can and should be activated just like *agapao* is. Rather, grace (*charis*) as referenced by the apostles is an action of unmerited favor. It is something God does "for" us. And something we do "for" one another. Grace carries no hope of reciprocity. It's the proverbial one-way street. We give without expecting any gift in return. Grace (*charis*) is linear, not circular.

Saved by God's *charis*, which Jesus either conveniently forgot to mention or else did mention (blame inconvenient amnesia by all the Gospel writers?) is good news for us as Christian believers. Yet the Gospel Jesus gave us in those biblical red letters was not a linear but rather a circular Gospel. It involved God's *agape* and our own reciprocal *agapao*. This, to my new way of thinking, is the even greater good news proclaimed by Jesus himself.

Love (*agape*) is not what is done "for" but rather "with" us. Love, though risking an unrequited response, still remains hopeful of reciprocity. It not only endures all things but it hopes all things. Love actively invites a response. Though it contains the unmerited favor of grace, it asks a favor in return. It is circular, not linear. Hence, *"I give you a new commandment, that you love one another. Just as I have loved you, you also should love one another"* -- John 13:34.

Why does Jesus come representing God's *agape* with us rather than *charis* for us? Perhaps, at least in my own 3rd Awakening experience, it is because we humans created in his image have the same ability to love one another as God has in loving us. This extends, if Jesus is to be believed, even to his teaching about loving our enemies.

Consider what Jesus may have meant in saying, *"But love your enemies, do good, and lend, expecting nothing in return. Your reward will be great, and you will be children of the Highest; for he is kind to the ungrateful and the wicked"* (Luke 6:35). While acknowledging that our love of enemy may still go unrequited by our enemy, it will always be requited to us by God without fail. Jesus made sure to point that out to us. Repeatedly. Indeed, unrequited love is something God, through Jesus, also experiences "with" us as part of our human suffering and gross disappointment. God is the source of our completed reciprocity and atonement in what amounts to our work of salvation.

Please do not in reading this believe I am discounting our need for God's grace or our need to give grace to and "for" others, such as when we forgive those who have never apologized nor even admitted any guilt. Grace is an important part of Christian faith, but I'm not so sure it is the most important part. I don't see it as being the salvation part of our faith in Jesus Christ. That, I believe, centers around our belief in God's love (*agapao*) story as including our own love stories in at-one-ment, God's love not only for but with us. Circular. Reciprocal. As in the lifting of our depressed mood we need someone to do "with" us, not "for" us, so in rising above our impulse to fearfully and sinfully control others we need someone to overpower that impulse "with" us, not "for" us. Which is why we sing during Advent for the coming of Emmanuel!

I think of the apostle Peter, who also appears to have considered our salvation to be more of a circular than linear process. Something that involves our reciprocal gift back to God rather than God's one-time action for our behalf. After all, his words *"For Christ also died for sins once for all, the righteous for the unrighteous, that he might bring us to God"* – I Peter 3:18 were preceded by these words, *"To this you were called, because Christ suffered for you, leaving you an example, that you should follow in his steps."* -- I Peter 2: 21. Could not Peter have been referring to the moral example where Christ's crucifixion was concerned? Or a few verses later, we read in I Peter 2:24, *"He himself bore our sins in his body on the tree, that we might die to sin and live to righteousness."* Of course, nothing of Peter's words speaks as loudly as Peter's actions when he, too, was later crucified as an early Christian martyr. No one took up his own cross after the moral example of Jesus any better than Peter.

> *Must Jesus bear the cross alone,*
> *And all the world go free?*
> *No, there's a cross for everyone*
> *And there's a cross for me.*

Could it not be that Jesus died for our salvation by setting the example "for" us to follow? Is it possible that we are saved by faith in God's love story not for us but rather with us as we follow him to the cross?

This best explains my reasoning from the experience I call my 3rd Great Awakening, the basis of which is biblical authority supported by our earliest of church traditions. This includes the Jesus-follower named Stephen in Acts 7. Where the cross is concerned, Jesus was right. We are saved not by "his" cross alone but by taking up "our" own cross in following his *moral exemplar*.

Leading up to the *moral exemplar* work of Irenaeus, the 2nd century Church father, was then the teaching of Jesus himself. After which came the writings of Paul who, lest we think wrote only of the *charis* God gives for us, also called the church to be like Jesus and join with him in *agapao*. Consider these powerful words from Paul's letter to the church of Philippi re. the example of Jesus:

"... be of the same mind, having the same love (agape), being in full

accord and of one mind. Do nothing from selfish ambition or conceit, but in humility regard others as better than yourselves. Let each of you look not to your own interests, but to the interests of others" -- Philippians 2:2-5.

In accord with my 3rd Great Awakening, I now accept Jesus as mentor rather than martyr. As such he calls me to learn from and follow his example of *agape* love and its own altruistic value in laying down my own life after the model of the cross. Jesus, as mentor not martyr, demonstrates for me a mindset of holy obedience to the Holy Spirit within. I reason from biblical authority using these words from Paul's continued letter to the Philippians: *"Let the same mind be in you that was in Christ Jesus, who, though he was in the form of God, did not regard equality with God as something to be exploited, but emptied himself, taking the form of a slave, being born in human likeness. And being found in human form, he humbled himself and became obedient to the point of death— even death on a cross"* (Philippians 2:5).

For Jesus, his own "lowest self-esteem" and his fear's heaviest stone would be death upon the cross. I believe he shared this "with" us that we might share in the saving power of love's resurrection "with" him. Salvation, then, is the atonement we have "with" the God who has faced our own worst fears, shared our temptations to take control, backed down from arguing with his own mind against the higher power of his own soul, and set the example for us of how to use loving influence to save us from our sins of fearful control.

1 http://www.pdhymns.com/pdh_main_M.htm

CHAPTER ELEVEN

Love's winning influence

"Setting an example is not the main means of influencing another; it is the only way."
- Albert Einstein

Before moving forward with some ideas about how my own nation might participate in what could amount to a 5th Great Awakening in the ensuing years, I'd like to summarize the contents of my own personal 3rd Awakening. I would like to also clarify the process by which I believe such awakenings occur, whether in individuals or in larger societies.

All Great Awakenings, I've come to believe, begin with fear. Fear is simultaneously felt in the body and known in the mind. Our human minds are tasked with then deciding what to do about such fears. Before making such decisions, our minds when used to our full creative (I believe God-given) capacity will test reality and gather information from our soul as well as our body. When our soul's information is then believed, our minds are awakened to a higher power within us. This amounts to the mind choosing to place more faith in love and more doubt in fear for a change. Such awakenings can then lead to much more effective decision-making, whether we are choosing in matters of personal or even national direction.

Social research in the United States reveals an increasingly large number of persons who view our nation as heading in the wrong direction. If a critical mass of persons seek re-direction, I believe it is possible to repent and turn in a different direction. My belief is based on my own experience, knowing that my own repentance has produced my own new awakenings. Sometimes there is no substitute for experience when it comes to reason.

In the process of my own three Great Awakenings, fear has proven to be the catalyst for change. As referenced earlier, I came to my 1st Great Awakening during my teenage years. Despite what I now consider to be a privileged upbringing, I was in my teenage years anxious about a number of deeply personal issues. As with most adolescents, I had some worries about belonging in a larger society, not just my own family. In my young body and mind, one

such larger society my senses were often stimulated by in my very
religious world was called "heaven."   Christians, my ears had heard
and my eyes read, "belonged" in this celestial society if they
confessed their sins and openly accepted Jesus Christ as Savior
through his death upon the cross.   That became step one of my 1st
Awakening as I took my place among my peers standing beneath
that old rugged cross on the slopes of my Rocky Mountain Summer
Church camp as a young teenager.   My earliest Christian faith was a
faith in fear, meaning that I was so afraid of instead belonging in hell
that my mind was finally opened wide to a new faith in love, albeit a
conditional love by God based on my praying the right prayer in
front of that old rugged cross.

A ways further into my teenage years brought to mind some
renewed fears in my body and mind having to do with my assured
belonging within earthly society.   Somehow belonging in heaven
after death had not absolved me of needing to also belong here on
earth in some adult role outside my immediate birth family. Heading
into my college experience without a clear sense of occupational
direction, I would hear and see my peers choosing various lines of
occupational endeavor.   I felt a need to belong in an adult world
with some occupational role in which to function.   Hence, step two
of my 1st Awakening as a 17-year-old was my call to professional
ministry while standing at the upper landing of Red Rocks
Amphitheater during a Christian Gospel concert. There as I looked
up into the starry Colorado sky and down into the city lights of the
world, my own purpose driven life took shape within my mind.

While that 1st Awakening carried me through college and into
grad school at United Seminary, it didn't stop other fears from
forming in my body and mind as I moved through the final turbulent
years of 1960's America.   Belonging to a society of conservative
Christians who were, at least in my own mind, on the wrong side of
history while supporting the Vietnam War and opposing the
American civil rights movement, is what triggered a whole new
round of fear within me.   The Christian church's pastoral ministry
became the place where I then knew I did not belong. Not if it was
turning a blind eye to the injustices within our own public policy.

Accordingly, this is where I then felt fear itself directing me
to leave the church and leave seminary in pursuit of a different
graduate degree and a more secular work in mental health
counseling.   I have been hesitant upon looking back to ever call this

some kind of new awakening or other conversion. What it did was place that 1st awakening in my rear view mirror. This produced a kind of lateral shift in career pursuits from Christian pastor to clinical therapist as a means toward helping other people find some larger hope and happiness in life. My mind was fairly quick to conceive of it as secular but still vocational ministry.

In fact, my mind settled into a fairly stable pattern of decision making across the span of my next thirty years. Naturally, I still had my fears and considered them to be an important source of information from the world around me through my bodily senses as I made my daily decisions. My body did come on too strong at times, such as in my mid-life crisis when I seemed afraid that I had not yet accomplished enough with my life, not yet made enough money, or not yet achieved a high enough status professionally. There again, for what my own mind can now conceive in retrospect, my body's information echoed shouts of the world around me telling me what I "should" be and "should" do as a man. Emotions of fear followed in those areas where I wasn't keeping up with the world's assorted "shoulds" in my life. At which point, my mind decided on various occasions to pursue different clinical jobs or at least different training opportunities to advance my resume. Still no great awakening there. Just a continuation of life within a normal human framework. More, I would now say, like a fear of falling behind.

What I later attributed my 2nd Great Awakening to was the family crisis precipitated by my brother-in-law's murder of his three young children. The death of my precious nephews and niece were the driving force that placed me back in seminary and in position for that second awakening. The best way I can think to describe that crisis is that it drove my fear to a level where it virtually shouted to my mind "take control" over other people. Enough with meeting them in the counseling office. I would need to meet them in the parish sanctuary. Counseling individuals was no longer enough. To gain control over my world then in crisis, I would need to preach to hundreds at a time. Micro interventions could not achieve meaningful control over this world's problems. Taking control to relieve my fears would mean a macro intervention through the Christian Church as a cultural institution. Such was more typical of my self-talk during that period of heightened anxiety about life and death.

Upon returning to seminary a door was opened for my mind

to grasp a very different love story acting as a higher power to my body's own fear story. This love story led me in the direction of servant evangelism within my local congregation. As a student associate pastor in my mid 50's it was like I was back in my 20's again, energetically organizing teams of servants from the parish to visit the sick, feed the hungry, clean toilets in strip shopping centers, hand out ice cold waters and cokes along street corners or parade routes, and more. All without any greater fanfare than to say, when invariably asked why, "it's what we think Jesus would be doing if he were here with you today." The closest I came to preaching in those days was saying "because God loves you in practical ways" when asked why I wanted to pay for parking meters, loads of laundry, or beverages at the drive-through. But this was enough to newly awaken me. I refer to this as my 2nd Great Awakening, even as it coincided with my very different understanding of what Christians call salvation. God's love, in my new way of thinking, was like the "payment" of ransom so we as God's kidnapped children could all return home immediately. Keep in mind this was concurrent with my country's terrorist crisis on 9/11/01, which had also become my next family crisis to deal with.

It is important to note that my return to United Theological Seminary 30 years after leaving it in 1970, though in some ways a starting over academically for me, was a refresher in dealing with the varieties of Christian thought throughout the first two millennia. Church historians had made but a few more footnotes over the years, yet significant advances were made even from 1970-2000 in piecing together theories about God, sin, and salvation or atonement. Hence, my systematic theology by this point took on a more postmodern worldview as well as a more feminist biblical hermeneutic. By my own Methodist reasoning, my thirty years' worth of further life experiences, when added to the church's expansion into areas of further orthopraxy, enabled me to better resonate with the authoritative biblical message. Servant evangelism, as developed out of the Vineyard tradition from what I regard as our nation's 4th Great Awakening on the streets of Hollywood, typified the church's expanded orthopraxy. Random acts of kindness among strangers on city streets were hardly the norm for Christian evangelism back in 1970. By 2000 they were front and center in areas of Church growth and evangelism. By 2005, I had helped bring about 150 new members, most by profession of faith, into our congregation of just under 800.

Moving on from those early years of successful parish ministry even after finally getting that long-awaited M.Div. degree in 2002, I found myself turning my back on this 2nd Great Awakening in ways reminiscent of that 1st Great Awakening many years earlier. As our nation plunged itself into another foolish war that to my mind was perhaps even worse than Vietnam due to its predictably destabilizing impact on the entire region of Shia Persians and Sunni Arabs, I developed a greater sense of fear once again. Once again I found the church to be practically complicit in support of this unjust war, and my bodily fear seemed to demand again that my mind decide to take control in reaction to our chaotic world. After the US elections of 2004, I chose to request a parish appointment beyond associate pastoral ministry in order to become a lead pastor in a different local church in 2005. My mind was then back in "fearful control" mode. Again felt like it was up to me to "change the world." And other nonsense.

As alluded to earlier, I found out that control is the last thing lead pastors can expect to have within their parish. What was worse, I discovered first hand that the more control I attempted to have, the less influence I was able to have. This forced my mind to pay much greater attention to my soul's perspective, and brought me back to the life of Jesus as an example of one with enormous influence in our world. Yet, this same Jesus surrendered all manner of control in relation to Caesar's tax collectors on one hand and his heavenly Father on the other. His rendering unto both Caesar and God confirmed that he was not the decider but the doer. The Father's decision to have this Son (body) of God "drink the cup" of crucifixion was starting to become clearer in my own mind. It was a decision informed by the Holy Spirit (soul) of God in the form of a love story that would triumph over the Son (body) of God's own fear story. Such a unique triumphalism was not aimed at any kind of penal substitution nor payment of ransom. It was only aimed at placing love's influence above fear's control when it came to this world's salvation from sin. And it was aimed at employing God's own body as the moral example of how we, too, should take up our cross, let go of our fearful control, and receive this same power of love's resurrection to roll away our own fear's heaviest stone. In this way, we would receive what I came to call a Post Traumatic Peaceful Order (PTPO) on this side of death.

Beginning with this second decade into the new millennium, I found my own mind's decisions more consistently informed by what I now call heavenly influence through my soul. I experienced this as my own higher power helping my mind comfort my fearful body. My mind became aware that my soul's desire for influence carried far more truth than did my body's demand for control. My mind still listened to my body the way a parent listens to his child, but by explaining to my "inner child" how love was more truthful than fear, how heaven's whispers were more truthful than the world's shouts, and how influence would always outlast control, my body began to relax. My newly relaxed body began making fewer demands for control, and learned how to say "nevertheless, not my will but yours be done" after the moral example of Jesus Christ, like never before.

Around that same time, I heard a story of someone else's loving influence in this world during the reign of Valerius Licinius in 4th century Rome. I presumed the story to be mere legend, but its power within my mind remains as profound as if it were literally true. I first heard the story through song, a lengthy ballad recorded years earlier by Tom Green. It had to do with a Roman jailer named Agleus stationed with his Army legion at a place called Sebaste just south of the Black Sea.

As legend has it, there were 40 soldiers in this large Roman legion that had converted to Christianity and were refusing to now pledge their worship and sacrifice to their Emperor as the one true god. The legion's commanding officer was worried that this group of Christians might pose a threat to the larger Army's command, and out of intense fear he decided in his own mind to take control immediately. The jailer Agleus was ordered to gather these forty soldiers together for a meeting with the commander.

Sebaste was having at that time an unusually harsh winter. The Sea was frozen near the shore, the harsh winds causing all soldiers to seek shelter in their barracks. Temperatures were far below freezing. As the forty soldiers appeared before their Army commander, they were compelled to renounce their Christianity and resume immediately the worship of their Roman Emperor.

Not one of these 40 soldiers was willing to obey.

It was the commander's decision that, to gain control over this apparent mutiny in the ranks, all 40 of these Christian soldiers would be taken by Agleus and his aides and assembled as a unit out on the frozen ice of that Black Sea coastline. There they were to surrender all manner of uniform and personal clothing upon the shore. Every item. And then march in formation onto the ice where they were to remain while reconsidering the matter of their Christianity. If upon changing their minds they were now ready to come back to the worship of their true Emperor, they would be escorted into a warm bath house nearby to save them from freezing to death by hyperthermia.

As the long minutes turned into hours, the men began falling first to their knees. They began singing and praying aloud. Steadfast. In unison. Refusing to save their own lives by returning to shore and entering the warm bath house to renounce Jesus. As the story continues, one soldier finally breaks. Under the torture of that frozen lake in winter, he turns toward the shore. Back he crawls. Slowly he tries to stand. Stumbles. Finally, he's able to make it back to where Agleus himself opens the door for him to enter that warm hut from which hot steam was pouring forth its life-saving powers. There he lowers himself to this time kneel in worship to the Emperor. It was as if this one soldier had decided upon a different faith. A faith in fear. And in such fearful control he had changed his mind in order to save his own life.

At which point something amazing happens.

Agleus, the jailer, has his own change of mind. While watching this entire act of torture taking place, it was as if God's loving influence was newly awakening his own mind through some higher power within his own soul. Drawing him forward. Forward to the remaining 39 men out on the ice. For as the one soldier had entered the warm bath house, so Agleus now left it. Piece by piece, garment by garment, he removed his uniform. Dropped every item of clothing upon the frozen ground. And out he marched himself to join in faith with these other 39 men on that frozen lake, surrendering his own life to follow Jesus Christ. The number was now restored. There were once again 40 brave soldiers for Jesus, dying a martyr's death to advance God's truest of all love stories in which they played a now prominent role.

It was this story that gave the final push to this rebirth I now call my own 3rd Great Awakening.

Whether it literally happened as told or became only the stuff of mere legend, the Agleus story affirmed something I knew about the human mind from my decades of working in mental health

counseling. Cognitive restructuring happens when the mind gathers
information from two conflicting sources and chooses that which is
more true. In this way we live into the truer and better narrative for
our lives. Space is created for doubt in our fear story and its glaring
falsehoods. And for faith in our love story and its newly glowing
truths.

In our fear story we are atoned with the world. We play a role
in the world's own fear story. The world finds itself out of control
and seeking human rescue. This world appeals to our human minds
through our own bodily senses. Take control now! Control over
chaotic or unfamiliar circumstances by means of fight of flight.
When we take up the world's cause, becoming "of" that world
within our dominant culture, we participate in fear's larger self-
fulfilling prophecy.

Such a fear story invariably begins with a verifiable truth
within our reasoned experience. Yet this foundational truth,
however solid it first appears, is ultimately proven to be a half-truth.
The rest of it is made up of lies and falsehoods.

God's love story begins and ends with the whole truth and
nothing but the truth, revealed in body (Jesus Christ) as well as soul
(Holy Spirit). Through this love story we are at-oned with God.
We become "in" the world but not "of" the world. We are atoned
with the God who, given the moral example of the crucified Christ,
lovingly surrenders all temporary control over worldly
circumstances in exchange for that which is far more truthful and
powerful: lasting influence. Heaven appeals to our minds through
our own soul's spiritual awareness, a whisper from heaven that can
so capture our attention away from even the shouts of this world that
we discover our truer story even amidst the world's chaotic or
unfamiliar circumstances. Our ultimate love story.

I wonder if this is not where Paul was going when he penned
these words to the Romans as found in the Christian New
Testament: *"I appeal to you therefore, brothers and sisters, by the
mercies of God, to present your bodies as a living sacrifice, holy and
acceptable to God, which is your spiritual worship. Do not be
conformed to this world, but be transformed by the renewing of your
minds, so that you may discern what is the will of God—what is
good and acceptable and perfect"* -- Romans 12:1-2.

What we in the counseling community call cognitive
restructuring is really a transforming renewal of the mind. It is a

choice to face this world's unproven future by faith not in fearful control but rather in loving influence. One faith turns out to be more false and the other more true. One faith contains the greater reality even into eternity, long after the world's shouts are exhausted and the body's fears forgotten. Which may be what Jesus most had in mind when stating that we cannot serve two masters (Matthew 6:24). One will be around forever and the other will soon fade away.

It is important to state once again that the body and soul are not always in conflict. More often I'd suppose they are on the same page upon informing the mind's own decisions. But when there is conflict, it is likely over which of these two great forces of fear and love is truer and greater. Our minds may have a default setting to gratify our body instead of our soul, but nothing so rewards our body than the heavenly love that has power to cast out our body's fear. In so doing we are empowered to change the world that then seems strangely less powerful over us. And we are freed to assert our own loving influence in the empowerment of others.

Amidst my 3rd Great Awakening, my own mind has chosen its own faith to be in love, because God is love. God, whose body faced fear's heaviest of all stones and then surrendered to his mind in that Garden of Gethsemane, is faithful in love. God's own Holy Spirit brings this same Godly and heavenly love to mind through our common soul. And amidst our own fear story, God restores or re-stories us by means of God's own higher power and author-ity.

It is not that I no longer have fear in my life. For as long as my body is alive, my senses of sight, sound, touch, smell and taste in reaction to this world will stir my fearful emotions in mind. My mind will listen attentively to my body as a parent listens to a child. But my mind will then decide based on input from my soul as well. Trusting that my soul speaks a wiser and truer story. A story of greater hope. Of greater power. Greater influence "in" but not "of" the world. Greater influence "with" but not "for" those who are now feeling powerless over fear's heaviest stone in their own world.

So where to from here in my personal life?

In no respect do I consider where I am now in my faith journey to be my destination. Nor do I expect to ever be entirely freed from fear. If I see, hear, touch, smell, taste immediate life-threatening danger, I expect my soul and body to both agree and inform my mind immediately using the same message. But where my body senses dangers my soul knows to be unreal, I expect my mind to learn increasingly helpful ways to hear my soul and reassure my body.

I have a very long way to go along my journey. Perhaps even a 4th Great Awakening will be necessary. I will go only as far as I can see, and when I get there I will be able to see farther. I am pursuing an identity with the apostle Paul whose own personal transformation and mental renewal resulted in these words of testimony: *"I have been crucified with Christ and I no longer live, but Christ lives in me. The life I now live in the body, I live by faith in the Son of God......"* -- Galatians 2:20 (NIV). That, to my current way of thinking, sounds like a much truer love story for me to live into. It certainly seems worth pursuing at this point.

CHAPTER TWELVE

Can the nation re-awaken?

"Love takes off masks we fear we cannot live without and know we cannot live within."
--James Arthur Baldwin

To this point, I have shared my views about what America's cultural historians often refer to as our three Great Awakenings (plus what I personally consider to be the 4th awakening that followed our tumultuous year of 1968). Some have suggested still other such awakenings over the course of American history and may be entirely correct.

Also, I have related my own history of awakenings at a more personal level. I have tried noting a similar pattern in all such Great Awakenings whether national or personal in nature, suggesting an issue of fearful control takes place within such patterns. I have suggested that faith itself first builds in the direction of some actualized "fear story." Out of such a narrative arises a new necessity. Out of necessity grows new invention. And inside this new invention lives an actualized love story that ends up overpowering the older and less truthful fear story. Our faith then shifts away from fear and toward love's truer story for our lives. We discover our better selves. We are then free to live our best lives and conduct our personal best practices.

I have noted as examples of this pattern those original disciples of Jesus who were newly awakened into love's influence after their own fearful control passed its tipping point following Christ's crucifixion. As the body of Jesus lay in the tomb in between that dreadful crucifixion and the day we now call Easter, a giant stone was rolled across that tomb's entrance. In a sense, I believe, that stone represented the heaviest possible fears those disciples could ever experience. Accordingly, Sunday's resurrection began a Great Awakening which lasted the remainder of their lives and launched the faith later labeled "Christianity" within this world.

But, oh, that frightening Saturday before. Those disciples spent that day hiding in a locked room perhaps waiting for the sound of foot prints outside the door belonging to those same Roman

centurions.   Every sign of impending post-traumatic stress had to
have been present.

Fear has a way of demanding that our minds take control of
the world on behalf of our bodies.   When that fearful control is not
possible, when all seems out of control, we are prepared to then and
only then accept the alternative of love's influence. Only when faced
with an unmovable stone, fear's heaviest of stones, are we able to
accept the new reality of love's resurrection in our lives personally
or collectively. Love's resurrection then has the power to roll away
fear's heaviest stone.

If, as I contend, fear must dominate the narrative before a
new awakening can occur, then my own country, the United States
of America, is perhaps close to another Great Awakening. As
recounted earlier in chapter four, this nation has a pattern of fear
stories building to crescendo over time that then result in some new
spiritual conversion or religious awakening.   As one's national, or
personal, fear story exposes its own failure, love's preferred story
comes along and exposes fear's falsehood. Which is when the
prodigal essentially "wakes up" and goes home. *"But when he came
to himself he said, 'How many of my father's hired hands have bread
enough and to spare, but here I am dying of hunger! I will get up
and go to my father'"* -- Luke 15:17-18.

So now the question: Can the United States of America, my
homeland, wake up and go home again?   Or borrowing that initial
example of Nancy Thomas from my days as a Traveler's Aid
caseworker, can we get the courage to hop off the back of this crazy
motorcycle and run away this time to that very home we at first ran
from?

I ask this question at a point where our own fear story has
exposed its own failure. In our most recent Presidential election, our
senses were overwhelmed by "fear of the other" messages
throughout every form of media.   Many of our citizens voted their
fears to one extent or another. So afraid of one candidate that they
voted for the other. Or stayed home for fear their votes wouldn't
make any difference.   Never in my seven decades of life in this
nation have I witnessed this level of fear in our people. "Fear of the
other" would dominate our narrative if our national story were to end
today.

But I believe America's story is not yet over.

I believe we have room for another awakening, or several

more awakenings, and that we can help each other create a better reality than this. We can collectively discover our better selves. And help each other live out a much truer American story. A love story.

There is no denial on my part, or perhaps your own, that the USA homeland is now bitterly divided. Economically. Politically. By gender. By race and ethnicity. By religion. By geography. By age. By education. We are a house divided against itself. But the United States had been divided against itself before, yet lived to tell the tale. Indeed, humanity at large has survived divisions throughout a history far deeper and wider than our own in America. Divisions sown by fear have resulted in restorations reaped by love. Fear stories have long been transformed into love stories where division melts into the arms of reunification.

Here is but one example.

It is a story involving a people once deeply and most bitterly divided. In fact, these people formed two very separate but neighboring countries. The sovereign nations of Korea and Japan. This particular story is told by Korean Christians, who begin with their own account of how their nation has long battled foreign occupation. Though each occupation army and government has been cruel, perhaps the greatest cruelty of all came at the hands of the invading Japanese after the turn of the 20th century. Many Korean victims of Japanese torture and abuse in that period left a legacy of fear that has tormented subsequent generations. This was especially true within Korea's Christian community, which was targeted with some of the most extreme incidents of Japanese abuse.

One incident in particular stands out for its barbaric quality and its trail of tears and then fears extending from a particular incident when military orders by the Japanese invaders were given to board up Christian Churches and to deport all foreign missionaries. After those orders were accomplished, the Korean Christians were silenced except for one native pastor. He took it upon himself to make pleas repeatedly for the Japanese police chief to allow his church to be reopened for worship. Humbly, and endlessly, he persisted.

Finally, permission was granted. Locks and shutters would be removed. All could gather for a single worship service inside their sanctuary. One more time this next Sunday morning. No promises beyond this one time.

The Christian community got the word out far and wide.
Christian families were invited to gather. And they did, even before
dawn on that new Sabbath morning. As they arrived, they were
forced to pass by the staring eyes of their Japanese captors, yet even
this could not dampen their spirits or quiet their joy.   They felt far
more excitement than apprehension or fear. And they filled the
wooden structure's small sanctuary to capacity. They were more
than anxious to praise their God with their own expressed cries of
Hallelujah!

Korean Christians have always loved the great old hymns of
the church, and that morning was no different from all the rest
except in volume. They sang more loudly, more spirited, than
perhaps ever before, it would seem. So loudly that they attracted
much attention from even the non-believing peasants in the
surrounding community. It was these peasants who then bore
witness to a gruesome atrocity.

As the congregation inside vociferously sang out words to
"*Nearer My God to Thee,*" the Japanese police chief waiting outside
issued an order. Immediately some officers began work on
barricading the doors so no one could escape. Other officers began
to pour kerosene all about the exterior structure. A torch was lit.
And the dry wooden skin of this small sanctuary quickly ignited,
sending flames and fumes within the building. Flooring, baseboards,
interior walls, all caught fire inside a period of several minutes.

Panic incurred. The worshippers began a rush to try the
doors.

No exit.

The windows. They would begin climbing out, only to
come crashing back in as their bodies were struck by bullets from
police firearms surrounding the church.

The good pastor knew it was the end.

With devout faith and confidence, he led his flock in one last
hymn of worship. It was a hymn whose words would serve a fitting
farewell to earth and a loving welcome into the presence of heaven.
Smoke burning their eyes, the congregation joined hands and arms
as best they could while billowing forth these words of song: 1

> *Alas! and did my Savior bleed?*
> *and did my Sovereign die?*
> *Would he devote that sacred head*

for such a worm as I?

Heartless Japanese officials and helpless Korean peasants now surrounded the building. Witnesses from the surrounding community came to the scene, some trying to help those inside but to no avail. They later told of seeing the little church's roof beginning its final collapse even as these words of that hymn's last stanza echoed their strongest statement of faith:

> *But drops of grief can ne'er repay*
> *the debt of love I owe:*
> *Here, Lord, I give myself away*
> *'Tis all that I can do!*
>
> *At the cross, at the cross*
> *Where I first saw the light,*
> *And the burden of my heart rolled away --*
> *It was there by faith I received my sight,*
> *And now I am happy all the day.*

Observers report hearing the dimming strains of music and wails of children amidst the collapsing roof and the roaring of flames said to consume every board and fabric within that sacred center of holy sacrifice. The souls who left singing finished their chorus in God's own heavenly center of resurrection. Indeed, love's resurrection had rolled away their own fear's heaviest stone, and God's spiritual exit was wide open despite all those earthly barricades.

The charred remains and rubble would go on to be removed from their community. But what the Korean peasants, victims' families, and a few Christian survivors could not remove was the feeling of hatred that burned on into the 20th century.

Decade after decade the pain lingered, the fire of anger consuming their memories of this traumatic incident. Where the victims suffered for merely minutes, their survivors suffered for many years on end.

With each passing generation, the elders would share the pain, and pass along the anger and the spite and the despair of rage itself. The monument built at the site would stand as a message to all who passed that they must never forget and never forgive this horrific atrocity.

Yet, this is not the end of their story.

Something would happen that would produce a saving change of mind. A change in terms of atonement. It would occur not because of the surviving faith brought by a suffering ancestry. Rather, it would have to do with a peculiar action of *agape* love, centered around the cross of Jesus, the atoning, restoring, reconciling Christ.

The change came about in 1972. It seems just prior to that a group of Japanese pastors touring South Korea came upon the site of a memorial to that atrocity. In fact, they were deeply touched with shame as they read from that memorial the names of these Christian brothers and sisters who had died at that scene.

Upon sharing this story among their own congregations back in Japan, there was a wider response of shame felt by these Japanese Christians in relation to their Korean brothers and sisters in the faith. Theirs was a new resolve to provide some Christ-like response in way of a love-offering. They raised among their respective congregations a total of ten million yen, then equivalent to roughly $25,000. They transferred this money through proper channels and a beautiful white church building was newly constructed on the site of that old tragedy.

As time arrived for the dedication service for that new building, a delegation of Japanese pastors and laypersons alike was sent to participate. They were politely acknowledged, yet they were left to sit predominantly across the aisle from where the Korean friends and family descendants of the victims were sitting. A kind of quiet tension was felt and the presence of Korean bitterness was unmistakable for these Japanese Christians now in attendance. It was as if the Koreans could not yet quite forgive their ruthless enemy's own descendants.

Enemy love is the steepest, highest and hardest hill for Christians to ever climb.

The service of dedication acknowledged the building's Japanese benefactors out of politeness. Hymns were sung and prayers were spoken. Other speeches were made. Details of the tragedy were recounted and the names of the dead were read and honored. More hymns were sung. And then the closing hymn: "At the Cross."

It is said that this is when the change began to occur, first among the Japanese delegation.

Tears began to form and then fill the eyes of these normally stoic Japanese Christians in the presence of the more naturally emotive members of this Korean congregation. As the singing continued, it was not long before weeping was heard from both sides of the aisle and the entire congregation was moved from positions of standing to, one by one, approaching those across that center aisle and embracing one another in an act of emotional solidarity and Christian unity.

At the cross, at the cross
Where I first saw the light,
And the burden of my heart rolled away ...

Japanese tears of repentance and Korean tears of forgiveness fell upon long awaiting shoulders until the site of that old nightmare was bathed in love. *Agape* love. Resurrection love as if rolling away their fear's heaviest of stones.

Happened there. In Korea. In 1972.

But can it happen in America? Now? Amidst our own divisions, our own hurts, our own bitterness?

My faith affirms that it can, but only when our own American "fear of the other" reaches some tipping point. Our current national anxiety level suggests to me this may not be too long of a wait. There is a growing burden of our hearts that will inevitably need rolling away in due time.

The common trajectory for fear to max out and love to move in follows, if my experience as a therapist is at all validated, something of an incremental course. Where our future uncertainties are concerned, by default we place our faith in fear's reality. We expect our fears to all come true. The good news is they never do all come true. The bad news is we never realize that until after our fears have all exposed themselves. That is when we see the light of truth in our lives. Only then, at our own cross, can we see the light that rolls away the burden of our heart.

Exposure to the worst possible scenario in our mind's imagination, at a personal level, means doing the very thing we fear the most. As if picking up our own cross and following Jesus. Something along the order of what those Japanese and Korean Christians did on that one special day in 1972.

At the cross, at the cross
Where I first saw the light,
And the burden of my heart rolled away ...

I can recall a client of mine in a counseling clinic I once worked in who had a dreadful fear of elevators. Our office was in a 7-story building. We were on the 6th floor, which means that client was able to get a nice little cardio workout going just getting up to our office by the stairwell. But the point is, the client may have skipped our appointments altogether if we'd been on the 12th floor of a 14-story building. This client was, as some might say, sick and tired of being sick and tired of not being able to ride an elevator anywhere.

This individual's fear was that the elevator itself would crash to the basement within its shaft and even exceed its top floor and go out the roof for lack of braking ability. Trusting the brakes this time wasn't enough to create trust in the next time.

Such solutions are never that easy.

So together we spent a solid 20 minutes, after walking down seven flights of stairs to the elevator basement, riding the elevator together from G (Ground) to 1 (1st floor). Up and down. The client was willing to risk crashing into the ground at the elevator's relatively slow speed, and willing to risk the brakes not working on the 1st floor by doubting it would reach the 7th floor on its own to exit the roof. So we rode up that one floor together. Then back down. Up. Down. Deep breaths in between. Twenty minutes. Seemed like an eternity, probably to both of us.

Then came the next twenty minutes.

From the 1st floor to the 2nd floor. Together. We made it. This time. Next time. Every time. (By the way, we were using a back elevator in a bank of three at a slow time of the day. After stepping off, quite often we could step right back on and reverse directions immediately. So we could make a lot of runs in just 20 minutes.)

Well, the next week it was more of the same. Client spent the first twenty minutes riding alone between levels G and 1. Then decided on trying G to 2 next. Then back down to G.

Just reading this you're already tired of elevators, right?

But the point is the client had to endure so many "next time" attempts that proved successful that faith in fear itself began to turn. A little doubt here. A little more doubt there. This doubt. Next doubt. Next doubt after that. And then the next. And a few weeks later the next ride with me from 1st floor to 6th floor, then down at the end of our session. Next week alone in the elevator. A couple weeks later another alone ride. Month later our next office visit. Then 3 months to the next session. Then 6. By that time, the client had even more faith in our elevator than in her own fear of elevators, which was really saying something! Next came another building's elevator when I wasn't around. Same drill. Ground to 1 and back. Ground to 2 and back. Ground to 3, 4, 5, 6, and in that case 7. And back.

That's the kind of trajectory I'm talking about with fear in general, whether faced by individuals or nations. Faith in fear may be our human default, but we can reset our default. We can learn to doubt our fear by doing the very thing we were afraid of and finding out it wasn't as bad as earlier believed or expected. As we come to doubt fear, we create space for our faith in love. That is the point at which love wins, and becomes our new default. It is the point I call love's resurrection. A Great Awakening.

It is reasonable to argue that facing our fears and doing anything at all we are afraid of requires some initial doubt when it comes to those fears. There is no fear we humans have that cannot be tested at some level. And no fear of even "next time" that cannot be proven wrong when granted a sufficient number of next tests. The key is to learn truth incrementally. Only then do fear's falsehoods give way to love's truth.

Few of us are unable to recall some fear that used to haunt us in the past but doesn't do so any more. We grew out of that one and perhaps several others. And we can grow out of today's fears just as well. Won't happen by running away. Will still mean having to face them as before.

Those of us Americans claiming to follow Jesus may take note of how Jesus faced his fear of going to Jerusalem. Spoiler alert: he went anyway. And he exposed his disciples to their own fear. He brought them along "with" him. Faced their fears together.

A curious thing, perhaps, is why after avoiding crowds threatening to kill him before, this time Jesus chose to do the very thing he was most afraid of: risk death itself by the Roman cross (crucifixion) in Jerusalem. The word "cross" first appears in the

Bible's New Testament (Greek word being *stauros*) when Jesus invites his disciples to take up their cross and follow him. Indeed, the very first mention in the New Testament of the *stauros* came in the context of Jesus preparing his disciples to go out in the world and do whatever he was doing. Following his moral example.

His disciples had already tried the easier stuff. (No, it wasn't riding the elevator from G to 1 with the therapist!) They had already gone door to door with a partner visiting homes of fellow Jews in Galilee who may need help in some tangible way. They had some success under their belt. But then, later in Matthew's 10th chapter, we read about a much bigger test upon the faith these disciples still may have had left where their own fears were concerned. *"And unless you are willing to take up your cross and follow me, you are not fit to be my disciples. If you try to save your life, you will lose it. But if you give it up for me, you will surely find it"* -- Matthew 10:38-39 (CEV).

Having started to doubt their own fears of going out on their own without him to knock on doors at homes nearby that weren't always welcoming, they were ready for a bigger test.   Hence, as over half of Luke's Gospel describes in much detail, the disciples made the trip to Jerusalem with him even though they were afraid of what might happen there. Along the way, Jesus had them travel by way of Samaria to face their fear of Samaritans. And then their fear of lepers. And then of tax collectors like Zacchaeus. In this way they learned that these "other" people weren't as bad as they had once feared. Little by little they were getting ready for the big fear they would face in Jerusalem.

Only then did Jesus expose them to their fear of death itself, fear's heaviest stone, so that his love's resurrection might raise doubt about the power of even death itself. And only then, on that original Easter, did his own disciples move past their still lingering faith in this world's fear story for their lives. Easter was their Great Awakening when fear came to be increasingly doubted and love trusted. Easter began as an introduction to their own heavenly love story by which their world's fear story was proven untrue. They were themselves saved not by any *penal substitution* or *Christis victor* or *ransom*. They were saved by following their Lord's *moral examplar*, taking up their own *stauros* and following him.

So what does this mean for America?

What it does not mean is that America is a Christian nation.

Nothing of the kind. It means instead that the people of the US are facing a cross or crossroad, metaphorically speaking, where we must choose to either avoid one another and run from our fears; or else face those with whom we are most divided. My own hope is that we will choose to face our fears, one small step at a time or one enemy at a time. As we do together that which we are afraid of, I believe we can start along the path to our next Great Awakening. Ultimately, fear will disappoint us all. Love alone will not disappoint.

A final point before moving on.

Fear itself believes in taking control. Love does not believe that at all. Love believes in giving influence. The difference is dramatic! Fear drives us to do things to or for others. Love draws us to do things with others. Fear is the information our world supplies our minds via our own body. Love is the information heaven supplies our minds via our soul.

We Americans will make up our own minds. Fear is now our default setting. We are free to do a reset, to change our own minds. And that is the best inalienable right our creator ever endowed within us as individuals.

1 http://www.pdhymns.com/pdh_main_A.htm

CHAPTER THIRTEEN

Can the Church again re-awaken?

"Love is what we were born with. Fear is what we learned here."
- Marianne Williamson

The late Christian author and educator, Phyllis Tickle, often struck me as being the church's best unknown futurist. I recall having an opportunity to speak with her a little while about her then newest book, *"Emergence Christianity,"* while at the Christianity 21 conference back in January of 2014. After she presented at the conference on that same topic, I recall having this overblown sense that meeting her would be like meeting Martin Luther 500 years ago. So I approached her, book in hand, hoping for an autograph but first just a minute or two of conversation about her views on the Church's participation in America's next Great Awakening. Ten minutes later I walked away happy to have met her but carrying away her book I totally forgot to get autographed. When Phyllis Tickle passed away in the fall of that next year, I deemed it a tragedy of lost treasure for the Christian Church, far beyond any small inconvenient absent-mindedness on my part in not getting her book signed.

Sometimes I am a bit too much in awe of mere mortals along my path. But that's not really the point.

There are times when the American Church seems to engage well with the surrounding culture and I think it's all about having a role to play in re-unifying and re-awakening our nation at large. Only to have this afterthought: the Church has forgotten to first unify and awaken itself. It's like we as that small-c catholic Church here in the United States have absent-mindedly forgotten something very important.

As critically minded as this will seem, I'm not sure today's Church isn't spreading more fear than love in our land. I'm not sure we're not at times more part of America's problem than solution. And I'm not sure how we're going to participate in America's next Great Awakening, as has been the case with such past awakenings, if we don't first wake ourselves up.

I doubt, however, we will fail to wake ourselves up. We may hit our snooze alarm a few more times, but my faith has it that we will eventually get up. And here is my vision of how that will then happen.

The Church in our nation will re-awaken and live into God's preferred love story for our life when we fully live out our baptism. It's as if today's Church claims a baptism we have already conveniently forgotten. Oh, we've remembered part of it. The rising with Christ part. But we seem to have forgotten that first part of our baptism having to do with dying with Christ. That's right. Facing our fears and dying with Christ. Being crucified with Christ is our *apriori* task before we can then claim resurrection with Christ. Or, said differently, we can't have an awakening if we've yet to even let ourselves fall asleep. First our crucifixion. Then our resurrection. Fully living out our baptism.

The remainder of this chapter will focus on what our crucifixion may look like in preparation for the resurrection I will cast a separate vision for in the next and final chapter.

Without argument, we may all find agreement that it was Christ's crucifixion that prepared the way for his resurrection. It was the apostle Paul's own testimony that the Christ would only live in him when he had died with Christ. *I have been crucified with Christ; and it is no longer I who live, but it is Christ who lives in me"* (Galatians 2:19-20). If we can all agree there was something like the heaviest of stones rolled across the inner blackness and hopelessness of Christ's tomb on that hill far away, then perhaps we can retrace the steps of our Lord leading up to that horrible event. And following there, by faith we will find our new awakening, God's preferred narrative of love's resurrection by which we can then help roll away America's heaviest stone in these difficult times.

Often times I think we've overlooked the fear factor, indeed the most human factor of all, in dealing with the experience of this Jesus we would all profess to follow. Yes, he overcame that fear, but I can't see how we can follow him out of the tomb in Easter victory if we don't first follow him into the tomb with our own fear and trembling. Perhaps this isn't far from what Paul was referring to when he affirmed the Philippians who would *"work out your own salvation with fear and trembling"* (Philippians 2:12). Jesus set a most important example of how to work out his own fear and trembling. A *moral examplar* we may far too often avoid following, if only by distracting ourselves with easier theories of salvation and atonement. He talked openly with others about the cross he was facing, and about the fears that came with it. Meanwhile, where our own fears are concerned, they seem to instruct us in the art of never letting others know of our own insecurities. We live by those farcical words taken from that fictional Hezekiah 1:1, "Never let them see you sweat."

You know what I mean?

Have you ever had a fear that you chose to just keep quiet about where your own church community is concerned? How about even when you're with your closest church brothers and sisters in the band, choir, class, or small group? Maybe do a "just pretend" even when it came to your fellow Jesus-follower? Or especially when it came to such persons? Ever think it is better to keep your worst fears away from the folks in your local church?

Wherever we've gotten such an idea, it surely didn't come from Jesus.

The synoptic Gospels all agree that Jesus did not just go privately into that Gethsemane upon the Mount of Olives, but he took with him Peter, James, and John. Matthew and Luke both concur with Mark, who wrote, that Jesus *"took with him Peter and James and John, and began to be distressed and agitated. And he said to them, 'I am deeply grieved, even to death; remain here, and keep awake'"* (MK 14:34). The expression of deep grief, *perilypos* in the Greek manuscripts, suggests something so severe in way of "peril" for Jesus that Luke goes on to use the metaphor of sweating drops of blood (LK 22:44) to describe him.

Jesus entered his time of crucifixion by first letting others see him sweat.

And fall upon the ground. And pray. No doubt with fear and trembling, or what some today would call having a panic attack rather publicly where these three disciples were concerned. Some of us know what that's like, whether as panic victims or else being in the company of such a victim. And so I wonder if we as Jesus-followers, his body the Church, do not need to enter our own garden of Gethsemane with our own witnesses at hand. Forget this "lone ranger" Christianity of the American west. Even Jesus did not "go it alone" where fear was concerned. He asked three friends to face it, his *perilypos*, alongside him. He made himself completely vulnerable. His earliest "charter" church members saw him sweat, making his own fear problem as transparent as at all possible. That's an example Jesus set for us to follow. His *moral exemplar* for our own saving work of fear and trembling as we follow him carrying our own most personal of crosses.

Years ago I completed a continuing education intensive in Narrative Family Therapy under the tutelage of Dr. Stephen Madigan at his office in Vancouver, B.C.   In principle, this mode of counseling treatment works at understanding two narratives that shape the life of each individual, or each family unit.   The first of these is labeled the "problem story" and the second is "the alternative story."   This approach borrows heavily from the post-modern views of a French historian named Michel Foucault. One of Foucault's many quotes reads in English, *"What is found at the historical beginning of things is not the inviolable* IDENTITY *of their origin; it is the dissension of other things."*   This suggests to Narrative therapists that greater truth is found beyond the foundations of what one might present as a "problem story."   Indeed, the "alternative story" may contain far more truth.   This is true of past stories we label "history" and of our own presenting stories of weakness or hardship.   Bottom line: there is far more to our own story than meets any eye.   The history of our own problem narrative most likely omits a much truer and stronger exception.   Such a problem-story often resembles a fear story others have seemingly written into our own history as if to define the truth of our being for us, thus omitting our many exceptions and strengths.   The point is, until we are willing to present our problem story and its associated fears, we can never really uncover our truer, alternative story and its associated love.   Put differently, we can't solve a problem we can't face.

That's a lot to think about, but try and stay with me here.

We are always more than whatever "worst time, place, and persons" are used by the world to tell our history.   To get at the larger truth, we must become our own author-ity and historian.   And so Foucault might have us resist those who claim the power to define us, those who claim to know our structure, our *"beginning of things,"* our identity or origin.   Though never expressed using this particular metaphor, we might all need to reset our default story or identity as set up at "the store" we've bought from in life.   We didn't come this way from the factory.   Someone else has activated or set us up.   And now we need to reset our own defaults, as it were.   Which is the aim of Narrative Therapy.

I've stated already in chapter 10 that my view of sin is perhaps best described as a spiritual auto-immune disease we operate

out of by default. In such a setting, our minds judge some facts to
be fiction and some fiction to be facts. We place our faith in fears
shared by the world through our bodily senses even though that very
faith makes us sick. We place our doubt in love as shared by heaven
through our souls, even when that love would make us well. In so
doubting, our mind instead attacks love's antidote to fear, as if love
is the false narrative and only our fear is true. This happens despite
the soul within us that re-minds us of love's power to heal and save.
It's as if God's Kingdom is already within us, but we tune a totally
deaf ear. By default, we trust only the shouts of this world to inform
our decisions. Love seems "too good to be true." So we are
socialized in our culture to follow the world's faulty directions for
our lives. Our sin is our failure to live a spiritually healthy life using
the heavenly wisdom and truth Jesus Christ lived by. We doubt the
love conveyed by heaven's truth as designed at the factory to inform
our own decisions. We choose to stay with the world's default
settings for our narrative.

The key point here is to consider how our mind trusts our own
body as perceived by our world, instead of seeing ourselves as God
sees us. In so trusting the world's impressions, we are prone to what
is sometimes called "body dysmorphia," a condition quit common in
relation to the disease of anorexia. And perhaps also common to the
Church, Christ's body in today's world. Upon lacking the "mind of
Christ" that Paul advised for the church, we see our body, Christ's
body, not as it really is but instead as the world perceives it to be.
We suffer from our own "body dysmorphia."

Here is an example of what I mean.

One of my greatest take-aways from my Narrative Therapy
work with Dr. Madigan involved a group module using what are
called "communities of concern" meeting weekly in his counseling
clinic. During the time I was there the trainers were mostly young
women meeting under the banner of "The Anti-Anorexia League of
Vancouver."   Each group member had been diagnosed with an
eating disorder, but by gathering together in that place, they were
agreeing to face their common disorder in support of an alternative
narrative each was striving to live into. Combined, they were a
resistance movement for truth and opposed to the lies Anorexia had
used to define them. Together, they were recovering from their own
"body dysmorphia."

I have been around quite a variety of different therapy and

mutual support or so-called "affinity" groups, but I'd never seen a group so powerfully effective as this one.   These ladies all faced a death-defying challenge: name their fear problem (anorexia) and lovingly bolster each other's immunity against that problem. Therapeutically speaking, their minds were empowered to understand both narratives and to choose the truer one to define themselves and restore, re-story, their own identities. In short, to change their own default settings.

For the yet uninitiated, the disease of anorexia acts to inform the mind of a vast array of lies that begin as half-truths.   These lies originate in one's culture and society. They are what I've earlier referred to as typical shouts from the world into our mind via our bodily sensations of sight, hearing, etc.   Partly the mind itself gets the world's messages wrong, but the other part is that the world's messages themselves are wrong.   The first part we would label "body dysmorphic," as when the world says "you are so skinny" but the mind believes, "you're just saying that because I'm still so fat and you're feeling sorry for me."   Hearing and accurately understanding what others are saying is important alongside seeing and accurately understanding what mirrors, scales, and medical tests are showing.   It's an insidious disease, and practically impossible to treat one on one. Its first lie is to "stay silent. Tell no one. Keep it a secret. They won't believe you if you say anything." Loosely translated: never let them see you sweat.

It takes a proverbial village working to support healthy hearing, seeing, and believing. Which is what this "community of concern" group in Vancouver did far better than most I've witnessed elsewhere. These were about 8-12 women working to monitor how their common problem story about death was seeking to fearfully control each other's lives that past week, and to affirm the times and ways in which that story was doubted and resisted. The group acted as a kind of social antibiotic attacking whatever lies were invading the bodies, and minds, of these young ladies. By spotting the lies anorexia had told each other in the previous week, they became a collective voice of doubt directed at those fearful lies.   Their group was like a powerful immune system that infused doubt into their respective fears, and faith in the love that was no longer "too good to be true" after all.

I found it quite amazing to observe how each person suffering from this deadly disease no longer had to depend on her own eyes and ears and understanding of the world's lying shouts of "thin" femininity and skinny jeans. Now there were multiple eyes, multiple ears, and multiple understandings applied to the world's threatening messages. One's own faith in fear could now be challenged by others who had many doubts about such fear. And from there the starved faith in the alternative story of love became the truer and stronger and fully nourished faith in life itself. Feeding each other the truth of love's dominant narrative was like a metaphor for the food each woman present needed to sustain life itself.

The disease of Anorexia itself serves as metaphor for those times when fear is like the fat we see ourselves full of while love is like the food we are starving for.

Many women in the "Anti-Anorexia League of Vancouver" were transformed through this process from their common problem story of death into love's story of new life. It was for them a Great Awakening. They could now doubt fear's lies and instead believe love's truth supporting their own preferred narrative. They could be empowered to define and to voice their own story.

And I remember thinking at the time. What if the Church were to work like this?

What if small groups of Jesus-followers were to meet weekly as "communities of concern?" To expose the lies our sin had used to most recently tempt us? Lies like, "tell no one. Keep it a secret. They won't believe you." Or "never let them see you sweat." Lies like "do be afraid" and "love ends" instead of biblical truths like "do not be afraid" and "love never ends." Lies like "you must take control" instead of truths like "when, not if, you lose control over others, you are free to then gain influence with them instead." Lies like "hate your enemy" instead of truths like "love your enemy."

What if the Church as a "community of concern" could face our common fears together and then become "communities of faith in love" instead of our adversarial "faith in fear?" What if we could confront our "body dysmorphia" together? Would that be the "community of faith" Jesus apparently had in mind for his own original disciples (charter church members)?

I can envision the Church gathering in small groups of four people called "Little Gethsemanes" where following Jesus would mean perfecting what the original disciples got wrong. That is, we would actually stay woke and be praying with each other. We would work out our salvation with fear and trembling together as "communities of concern". We would be authentic, vulnerable, gracing each other with the safety to sweat drops of blood in each other's presence. We would account for those times when the world, sin, Satan, or whatever word we choose, tempted us to trust fear this past week and to doubt love. When all four people have shared about those times, we would pray in some comfortable fashion to not "fall into" such temptation. Then, having prayed together, we would share together Christ's means of grace by which we would rise up in doubt to resist our fears, and in faith to restore our love. We would proclaim to each other the good news of truth and of love's resurrection power even to roll away fear's heaviest stone in our respective lives. We would redeem the Garden of Gethsemane that first let Jesus down so long ago.

The first rule of living out of a fear story: keep it to yourself. It's our little secret. Tell no one. No sweat. The first act of a re-awakened Church is to break that first rule by which sin enters our lives. The second act is to externalize or "cast out" this problem and replace it with the love that is not "too good to be true" after all.

Going back to my own premise that sin is essentially a spiritual disease, an auto-immune disorder in which the body commands our mind to take control instead of trusting the soul's healing antidote, it is most important for us to not identify ourselves as sinners.

Let me say that again. And this time with emphasis.

We. Are. Not. Sinners.

We would never say "I am a cancer" if we wanted to defeat our cancer problem. By identifying with our disease, the actual antidote then becomes the foreign object our bodies set about resisting. Sin, like cancer, is like a demon that enters our lives but does not belong here. It invades our goodness and our true identity. If I am cancer, then the treatment becomes my enemy.

By wrongly identifying with our sin, our truer "love story" becomes an outside foreign invader that we naturally resist or defend against. And not only do we reject this foreign object of healing salvation, we treat our own sin like a diseased limb we would prefer "never" to amputate. Or, upon such amputation, we would have a kind of "phantom sin pain" as if craving its return. And all because our identity is wrapped up in saying "I am a sinner." Which sets us up for the most natural of relapses. (I have similar thoughts about those who identify themselves as addicts such as alcoholics.)

What we learn from Jesus about healing the demon-possessed is most instructive when it comes to doing Church. Jesus confronted the demons, not the victims. He spoke directly to "it" or "them" and worked to externalize or cast out the problem, not the person. He named the demon something very different from what the person's own name was, so there could be no mistaken identities. And with other diseases, he identified blindness and leprosy by their names rather than by their victims' names. As would happen in Narrative Therapy, Jesus made clear that "you are not your problem. Your problem is your problem." You are good. Your true self is your heavenly soul. The foreign object entering your body and mind is from the world. That, not you, is your problem.

You. Are. Not. A. Sinner. You are holy but sin has gone viral and invaded you from the outside in, the world into your mind using your body as a vessel. Your soul and higher power is here to, in terms used by 12-step programs, "replace your old stinking thinking."

John's first epistle to the churches contained these important words, *"Children, you belong to God, and you have defeated these enemies. God's Spirit is in you and is more powerful than the one that is in the world"* (I John 4:4 - CEV). I believe John was lovingly influenced within his own soul to write these words, but I also believe John was following the moral example and verbal teachings of Jesus. It was Jesus who called the Church out of the world. *"If you belonged to the world, the world would love you as its own. Because you do not belong to the world, but I have chosen you out of the world—therefore the world hates you"* (John 15:19). Here Jesus was speaking to his disciples concerning their own future role as the *ekklesia* who were "called out" from the problem narrative of fear "and into" God's preferred, healthy, Kingdom narrative of love. A bit later in John's Gospel account, he quotes Jesus as saying, *"I have told you all this so that you will have peace of heart and mind. Here on earth you will have many trials and sorrows; but cheer up, for I have overcome the world"* (John 16:33).

I don't think Jesus has ever asked us to reject the world itself. God made the world good and intends for it to be a source of natural nourishment to our bodies and minds; yet, quite frankly our world has gotten sick and is a carrier infecting us as individual persons.

Jesus loved the world, and our bodies and minds, as a great physician. Love is the antidote to the world's most contagious and even paralyzing problem. Love empowers us to detach from the world's problems instead of identifying with them. Jesus saves and heals by casting out sins, not sinners. And he calls us into communities of concern that go and do likewise. He did so starting with the Garden of Gethsemane, where the weary members of his original church had to be repeatedly re-awakened.

As you can see, one of the problems I have learned through my own personal Great Awakenings to detach from is the world's problem of fear. I have named my fear problem "this sin" even as Jesus referred to his as "this cup." Like Jesus, fear has sought control over me by first commanding avoidance. The body commands the mind to fight or flee. Jesus similarly told the Father to let this cup pass from him. Avoidance is the truest evidence of fear. Common human experience. And Jesus was fully human "with" us when he came to his own fear's heaviest stone. The big difference is that Jesus made no command upon the Father but rather invited the Father's command over himself; *".... yet, not my will but yours be done"* (Luke 22:42).

Jesus gave his fear problem over to God's Fatherly mind for decision and deliverance. Deliverance from evil after he had been otherwise led into temptation. Yet, we as Jesus-followers too rarely tell anyone, God or God's people, about our own temptations. Unlike Jesus, we as his body today too often keep secret our fear problem. We quite literally are too afraid of our own fear. We avoid that which we, if following Jesus, should face up to and overcome. Unlike Jesus, we go to our own Gethsemane garden alone instead of taking along a group of our closest associates to pray and watch "with" us. And so we continue our "body dysmorphia" as the Church.

The 12-step movement has many catchy sayings that have inspired and influenced me over the years. One I will always remember is, "you are only as sick as your secrets." Although the Anti-Anorexia League did not operate as a 12-step group, they employed the same healing capacity to confront fear head on, call out fear's lies, and live into love's preferred alternative story.

That is my vision for today's Church in the United States.

If we are to be healthy, we must be honest with ourselves, and not only ourselves but then others. We must make ourselves vulnerable, transparent, emotionally authentic. Only then can we effectively love our neighbors as ourselves. Love's first core value is honesty for the sake of understanding, and then understanding for the sake of influence. None of this happens in isolation. It requires communion and communication.

The writer of Ecclesiasts puts it this way, *"Two are better than one, because they have a good reward for their toil. For if they fall, one will lift up the other; but woe to one who is alone and falls and does not have another to help. Again, if two lie together, they keep warm; but how can one keep warm alone? And though one might prevail against another, two will withstand one. A threefold cord is not quickly broken"* (Ecclesiastes 4:9-12).

True of persons. True of recovery programs. True of churches. True of nations. We will choke to death on our own secret sins. But we can re-awaken and live on with great influence when we come clean in admitting our own fears that have sinfully driven us to assume control over the world around us.

At this point, I think it is essential that I do more than assail fear as being a kind of sin or "control" issue in our lives at all levels. There is, after all, a reason why fear drives us to assume control and to thus oppose God's love story of non-controlling influence even though it is our truer narrative.

Sue and I, when nearing 50 years of marriage, decided to use our own love story in a way that might be a helpful influence in some other couple's lives. We designed a pre-marriage workshop we call, "The 4 Cs of the Marriage Diamond."

Not the engagement diamond. The marriage diamond. Where the rubber actually meets the road. Past the point of any Cut, Color, Clarity, and Carat. We measure lasting marital values according to these C's: Covenant, Compassion, Communication, and Character.

This "Marriage Diamond" is the investment that truly appreciates over time.

In our training module on Communication, our 3rd of the four C's, we note how it is that our assumptions get in the way of our better communications.

Here is a classic example of how that happens in marriage. A couple makes assumptions about anger and enters the land of unintended consequences by seeking control over an argument. Known as "getting the last word in." Sound familiar husbands? Wives?

I said unintended consequences.

As an old marital therapy professor used to put it, "we have to live with our consequences, not our intentions." And the consequence of our once made assumptions about anger is that we then fail to communicate about what is below the surface. Which is most everything else inside us as human beings. We stay angry instead of seeing what lies beneath and within. Anger is a surface emotion. As smoke is to fire, anger is to fear. Yet, we too often "assume" our marital conflicts are about anger. All I can say is "not really."

And here is where communication becomes critical to our success in marriage. Just as firefighting professionals would find their jobs hopeless if they went about trying to fight smoke and put smoke out by trying to control the direction of the wind, so couples feel hopeless and eventually ready for divorce upon trying to fight and extinguish anger by controlling the direction of an argument. Want to restore hope? Then fight fire instead of smoke, fear instead of anger.

Which is not to say anger, or smoke for that matter, must be ignored. It needs to be dealt with using a safety plan. Perhaps a time out. But anger is not the main problem; only the presenting symptom. Anger, like smoke, is what gets a couple's attention. Step one.

Then comes step two. What is the source of that underlying fear? What caused it before and what can cause it again? This is no different than a firefighter seeking to find the source of a fire.

Underneath every fear is a hurt. Hurt has caused a fear that has caused an angry "control" reaction to prevent further hurt. Yet, it doesn't prevent such recurrent hurt because underneath that hurt is an unmet expectation, some type of a deeper betrayal. Trust has been traumatized. Marriage-wise, here is where our faith in love turns to doubt, and is replaced by faith in fear where our future uncertainties are concerned.

But we're still not through communicating, are we? Still a long way to go.

You see, marital communication is like peeling an onion. Underneath our anger is our fear, underneath our fear is our hurt, underneath our hurt is our unmet expectations. And, if you're ready for this, underneath those unmet expectations are typically some unrealistic expectations. My frequent question for couples in marriage counseling goes: "Is it possible that some of your expectations for each other were unrealistic in the first place?" If so, there's usually a pretty good answer as to why. Some of our expectations for each other in marriage were never communicated. They were only assumed. We've forgotten to share them and to ask if our expectations of each other seemed realistic or not.

Kind of like my forgetting to get that Phyllis Tickle book autographed as first intended.

Now are you getting the picture?

Underneath our unrealistic expectations are our unspoken expectations, and underneath these are our unknown expectations. Often times, we haven't even known what to expect. We've not even had any self-talk on the subject.

Developmental psychologists have long attributed such tasks as marital intimacy to be preceded by those having to do with personal identity. This is why a failure identity almost inevitably leads to a failure of intimacy. If I don't know who I am as a person, or what to expect of myself, setting my expectations for the next person is in itself too much to expect.

So we have to sometimes peel that last part of our own onion. And this seldom happens without the shedding of tears.

Perhaps that is why "Jesus wept" also.

I have to wonder. Before Jesus approached the fear problem he shared with other associates in that Garden of Gethsemane, isn't it true that he wept over that same Jerusalem he would soon enter? And I wonder if he wasn't then feeling the hurt that came with the unmet expectations that his heavenly Kingdom would be well received and not badly rejected, as was about to happen. Perhaps Jesus had a fear problem that came from the hurt of his own people failing to meet even his own outspoken, not unspoken, expectations. I believe Jesus knew who he was, what he expected, and said so. But I believe he was hurt that even his own Hebrew people would not care, would not listen, would not meet his expectation for God's Kingdom to come on earth as it had in heaven. Even worse than that, they wanted him dead.

Who wouldn't have wept?

Jesus communicated effectively. But even communication is not an end-all. Rather, it leads into a question of character, which is the final point Sue and I discuss when presenting our 4 C's of the marriage diamond. When even communication fails, we must rely on our character. For it is our character that will re-awaken us to our covenant, and our covenant to our compassion.

The Apostle Paul had these words for the Church in Ephesus: *"Husbands, love your wives, just as Christ loved the church and gave himself up for her..."* (Ephesians 5:25). Could this not mean we are to follow the example of Jesus who, loving those disciples who would plant his first Church, let them see him weep? And face fear? And be seen to sweat drops of blood?

There is something about the communication of love within marriage that requires vulnerability. Emotional authenticity. Not only setting a loving example by making oneself vulnerable, revealing the depth of one's own distress such as we find Jesus doing with his Church's earliest "charter members" in that Garden, but one more thing of importance. Marital communication of love involves asking for vulnerability in return.

Looking at this point of Gospel reporting, we read in Mark's account where Jesus *"took with him Peter and James and John, and began to be distressed and agitated. And he said to them, 'I am deeply grieved, even to death; remain here, and keep awake.' And going a little farther, he threw himself on the ground and prayed that, if it were possible, the hour might pass from him. He said, 'Abba, Father, for you all things are possible; remove this cup from me; yet, not what I want, but what you want.' He came and found them sleeping; and he said to Peter, 'Simon, are you asleep? Could you not keep awake one hour? Keep awake and pray that you may not come into the time of trial; the spirit indeed is willing, but the flesh is weak'"* (Mark 14:33-38).

There's actually quite a bit to unpack here. Especially if we're talking about the Church's own re-awakening as the body and bride of Christ.

It seems in speaking about his own grief or distress, *perilypos* in the Greek, before throwing himself on the ground and begging the Father to change his mind, Jesus was casting an early vision for his Church. These earliest church leaders would live into a culture of mutual transparency and mutual support. Instead of being grieved alone, one would have a small group to remain "awakened" or woke together. Church people would suffer "with" each other. And why? That they *"may not come into the time of trial"* or be led into temptation.

Remember the Lord's Prayer? And that line about praying

to be led "not into" temptation? There Jesus uses this same word, *peirasmos* in the Greek, for both his prayer in MT 6:12, LK 11:4 and in his Gethsemane prayer-meeting of MT 26:41, MK 14:38, and LK 22:40. Staying awake together was necessary for not being led into his new Church's time of *peirasmos,* trial, and temptation. Necessary precisely because the body and spirit were not on the same page, as it were. The spirit was willing, but the body was weak. And the mind was forced to choose. As is always the case.

If this was indeed the vision of Jesus, a kind of prototype for what I came to observe as "The Anti-Anorexia League of Vancouver," then it is quite obvious his original vision did not take. Or at least not immediately. This small group support and accountability model Jesus introduced during his own time of greatest fear essentially failed to launch. Three times Jesus tried, but each time he found his church leaders all asleep at the switch. By this point, fear had already taken root. His arrest was at hand. And Jesus was left to do the only thing now possible: issue a wakeup call to his small church.

Perhaps it is time now for us to re-awaken as his Church and to redeem the Garden of Gethsemane, if only by four people at a time following that original moral example.

These words of Jesus, *"Get up, let us be going. See, my betrayer is at hand"* (Mark 14:42) contained much significance, I believe. The word for "Get up" is *egeiro* in the Greek. It means "rise" and is used interchangeably with another word, *anistemi,* whenever Jesus would talk about his own resurrection. It essentially meant rising from the dead, standing up, or even "awakening" from sleep. It conveyed a need for the church to rise and awaken at the very point when it is otherwise tired and afraid.

I see today's small-c catholic Church as being tired and afraid. And called by Jesus to follow his own example. To "get up" (*egeiro*) again, yes. To first be prayerful, of course. To be genuine with one another. Emotionally authentic. Vulnerable. Transparent. And to suffer "with" each other in our own distress or (*perilypos*). For in so doing, the Church can be a transformed and transforming change agent for the nation(s) by shifting from a dominant fear story over to God's preferred love story for this world he so loves.

So back to the original question: can the Church again re-awaken? Yes, but only if we get beneath our anger and openly communicate our fear, and then our hurt, then our unmet expectations, then our unrealistic expectations, then our assumed and previously unspoken expectations. Perhaps, for many, even our unknown expectations.

We as today's church must peel away our bodily onion of emotions and expectations.

Will there be tears such as Jesus himself wept? Yes. Will there be pain? Yes. Just like Jesus had in facing his own cross of *perilypos*. Which brought him to his own darkest tomb, sealed by fear's heaviest stone, and then to his own love's resurrection in final fulfillment of our one Lord's one baptism.

CHAPTER FOURTEEN

When the Church Re-awakens

"All truth passes through three stages. First, it is ridiculed. Second, it is violently opposed. Third, it is accepted as being self-evident." -- Arthur Shopenhauer

No one likes to end any book with a story of pain or hurt. Pain is the very thing that scares us and feeds our heaviest of over-weight fears. Yet, I've just suggested in the previous chapter that for the Church to follow precedent in support of our national Great Awakenings, there must be some new facing of fear and its underlying pain within our own body. Otherwise, the Church will lack credibility in responding to our national fear and pain. Our own hurtful times must be exposed. And our hurts forgiven. Only then will we qualify to help our nation with her own hurts.

The place to begin is with me.

Just as the Church may need to re-awaken before the nation can, so I must re-awaken before I can ever realistically expect the Church to do so. I must face and then expose my own hurt, fear, anger. I must die with Christ before I can rise with Christ. I need to follow him to the cross before I can then follow him to the Church. Because it is on my own cross that I will be able to forgive the Church and lower my own expectations going forward.

The first thing I must forgive the Church for is telling me that I am my problem, I am a sinner, and the world around me is innocent. I must forgive the Church for prioritizing Paul's teaching of grace (*charis*) above Christ's teaching of love (*agape*). I must forgive the Church for sending Jesus Christ to the cross "for" me and not "with" me. I must forgive the Church for, at least implicitly, expecting that my baptism meant rising with Christ without having to first die with Christ. I must forgive the Church for trying to fearfully control the world and thus avoid pain for ourselves as a body. Nobody likes pain. Everybody wants to go to heaven, but nobody wants to die.

I get that.

I forgive the Church for being human. I forgive humanity for being human. I forgive the world's activation of our human default setting for faith in fear and control in dealing with others, including

God. If I can forgive my cellular supplier for setting my phone's default in ways that I now have to go in and change for my own benefit, then I have to forgive the world for what amounts to the sin of fearful control that has robbed me of my loving influence.

There was a time prior to my 3rd Great Awakening where I'd have had to say I forgive God. That I must forgive God for not taking control over God's own creation in order to prevent human suffering.

That was back in the day, back over the many years even into my 60's, when I believed God's power came from his own might and his own might from his own knowledge of "everything," including the future. I spent my whole life up to that point believing, in error, that God's might makes God right.

And for that I have to now forgive myself for having believed a lie my body often heard the religious world claim was true.

My personal 3rd Great Awakening has helped me see God's power in a very different way. Basically, a whole new faith paradigm. I now see his power coming through his love. Not his knowledge, but his love. God's loving is what leads to God's knowing, not the reverse.

In other words, right makes might.

Yes, I used to believe that might makes right. That love is what one did when one knew everything about everything, the future included, and that love was what one did with who one is. Nowadays, I'm inclined to believe who one is must be defined by what one does. We learn, and we know, by doing. And the more we do, the more we then know.

Within the broader field of contemporary theology, one of the newer kids on the block is named "open theology." This is the belief that God, rather than knowing and controlling all things from the beginning of creation, knows and is still learning by doing. The more God creates and does, the more God then learns and knows. God's power follows after God's love. Right makes might. God is not finished learning and knowing, because God is not finished loving and doing. Creation, by its very nature, means "open" to new possibilities, or to "a truer narrative" than before. God of the "omnipotent not yet" cannot know everything because he has not yet done everything.

Living into God's preferred love story for my own life has meant re-awakening to a truer narrative than I could not know about before doing what I've most recently done in my life. And forgiving myself for knowing not what I was doing because I hadn't done it yet. Knowing follows doing. For me. For the Church. For the United States of America. Yes, even for God.

Turns out "live and learn" also makes for good theology. The living God is not through learning by doing. Nor as we as God's offspring.

If upon my 3rd Great Awakening, my new reasoning begins with the authority of scripture, I find myself drawn to this message from Jesus as reported in John's 14th chapter. In particular, *"Very truly, I tell you, the one who believes in me will also do the works that I do and, in fact, will do greater works than these, because I am going to the Father"* (John 14:12).

Consider this. Jesus is facing fear's heaviest stone, his own death on the cross. He is preparing the disciples for their loss of his presence and his power. And he is promising that they will do greater things, enact more loving influence in this world, after he dies than he could enact during his own lifetime. How? Because God's loving influence empowers everyone, not just himself.

Some would call this synergy. The Cambridge English Dictionary defines synergy as being "the combined power of a group of things when they are working together that is greater than the total power achieved by each working separately."

This begs a new question: what is more powerful than God? Answer: the power of God's people working together. Or in other words: God's unified Church. Make that: God's re-awakened and unified Church.

Now get this.

John's 14th chapter continues with Jesus telling his same original disciples, these charter members of his original Church:
  "And I will ask the Father, and he will give you another Advocate, to be with you forever. This is the Spirit of truth, whom the world cannot receive, because it neither sees him nor knows him. You know him, because he abides with you, and he will be in you" (John 14:16-17). Through Jesus, God enters the world with the power of one human body (the Son) under the direction of the one divine mind (the Father). Through the Church, God enters the world with the power of all human bodies under the influence of one soul (the Holy Spirit). Bottom line: God's mind (Father) empowered his own body (Son). God's soul (Holy Spirit) empowers everybody

(Church) to do "*greater works than these*" done by Christ alone. Divine synergy includes us, the Church of Jesus Christ.

It took me awhile to catch on to this. More than 60 years, if I'm forced to count. So I'm a slow learner. But I've learned by doing, by creating, by making my own mistakes along the way, facing my own fears along the way, losing my own failed battle for control over the other. Taking up my own cross. Following Jesus as my Savior and *moral exemplar*.

And if I can do it, so can the rest of Christ's Church.

And if the Church can do it, so can the now frightened and fractured United States of America. If this nation can do it, so can the whole world God is continuing to so love. There really can be a global Great Awakening. The one Jesus calls the Kingdom of heaven. No Near Death Experience required.

What is required involves some open exposure to our fears and hurts. And some loss. And doing what is right where that loss is concerned by giving our loving influence instead of taking our fearful control in the world. As we let go of our own kingdom and hold on to the one Jesus humbly took to the cross, we will gain influence wherever it is most needed. Right will make might. We will act our way into a new way of feeling, because waiting to feel our way into a new way of acting is always a fool's errand. We will know better after we do better. We will shift our paradigms and be re-storied into the light of God's preferred narrative. We will discover our better selves and so will the world around us. We will be transformed from hurt people who hurt people, which is where the Church too often is today, into hurt people who help people. We will be working smarter instead of harder. And we will be adding by multiplication.

Instead of the body dysmorphia with which the Church is too often viewed today, both internally and externally, we will grow to look like Jesus when we grow to act like Jesus, cross and all.

Losing and loss in life produces in us all a very new perspective. Perhaps even a new Great Awakening.

Losing requires us to look outside our customary box, to live outside our customary womb, and to only then find that "on earth as it is in heaven" experience of perfect love with no remaining fear of punishment and further hurt. To find out here and now what some have, through their own Near Death Experience (NDE), associated only with heaven then and there.

This is God's preferred love story into which we enter, leaving behind the world's default setting of fear. This defines for us our truer narrative. This delivers for us love's true resurrection, which then has the power to roll away fear's heaviest stone.

You may consider examples from your own story, or the stories of others. Bible stories and beyond. Perhaps even Church stories, if you are so daring as to explore further.

I have a Church story to serve as example. And I'll use it to close with. It's a story of transformation. About another Great Awakening. Which means it's not about how hurt people hurt people; rather, it's about how hurt people help people. It's about Mark and Beth Wenzel. People from my own local church here in Ohio.

As a young couple with two children and one on the way, Mark and Beth were committed Christians but only casually involved in the church. They began attending back in 1990. They came with the normal challenges of a young family, including a 6-year-old Aaron and his 2-year-old sister, Meghan. At the time of Beth's third pregnancy back in 1993, their pattern was to passively attend worship services while both kids were in Sunday School. Beth would sometimes assist their respective teachers. That was about it. Few of us even knew they existed.

Then came Alex, born on May 24, 1994.

Alex was born with a heart defect in his atrial-ventricular canal. In time he would need surgery to repair that defect.

The time came in October of that year, and the proper care was taken to involve a pediatric surgeon specializing in cardiac repairs. Alex came through the surgery very well, and his recovery over the next several days went well in the cardiac step-down unit. By all reports he was doing well enough to have come home on October 18th upon completion of a few further test results.

However, an unexpected crisis, perhaps a blood clot, occurred late into the evening of October 16th. He became unresponsive. All attempts to then save his life failed. He died in Beth's arms while Mark, after securing Aaron and Meghan with grandparents, was still en route from home some 60 miles away. All failed attempts at resuscitation were ended at 2 a.m. on October 17th. Alex was gone.

Instead of bringing Alex home from the hospital as planned for that next day, they would begin planning with a local mortuary for final arrangements. They would return home to crushed grandparents and stunned siblings. To be alone. Empty. Numb. Going through the motions of calling other family, friends, neighbors.

And calling the church.

First to arrive from the church to offer whatever mercy Christ himself might have dispensed, was Rev. Jack Drodge, Associate Pastor for Congregational Care. Jack was the kind of pastor who, on his day off, would volunteer to go to the local Children's Hospital here in Dayton and rock infants born with "crack-cocaine addiction." A better person for the task of helping the Wenzels could not have been found anywhere on the planet. Through him and another staff Associate, Rev. DeAnn Long, along with a local grief support group for parents like themselves, this family was empowered to face their anger, fear, hurt, unmet expectations. To face it all. And to be the hurt people these terrible circumstances naturally dictated.

If there is indeed good news, some silver lining, to be found in the devastating pain of losing an infant such as Alex, it is this: hurt has no power to author-ize anyone's life story. Derail it for a time, yes. Drive it into some dominate and permanent fear story forever, no.

Now, nearly a quarter century later, if one were to ask the average member, most of whom are new, inside our local church just who Mark and Beth Wenzel are, this would be the unwavering response. Beth is the Director of Children's Ministries for the church. She goes out of her way to assist new families, and to help their kids experience God's resurrection love. She influences many to overcome their own worst fears. Mark, a dentist by profession, would be identified as the head of our mission team to Barahona, Dominican Republic. Going on 16 years now! There "Dr. Mark" attends the most critical dental needs of an impoverished community from morning to night over the course of a week each year, a personal vacation week from his own dental office. Why? Because he is committed to helping the hurting. Along with these activities, the Wenzels are found throughout the church leading the work of various committees, assisting in various worship services, feeding the hungry and attending the needy far and wide. Mark is known for having helped start the church's health ministries and for then supplying them with a grief support group, which he and Beth were both involved in leading at the very beginning. And together Mark and Beth are known as the parents of three now successful adult children, their youngest being another daughter, Lauren, born two years after Alex's death.

The Wenzels are an example of what can happen when a church goes through pain. Deep pain. So deep that those who hurt the worst are automatically sensitized to the hurts not only inside themselves but then outside themselves. So deep that they are thus empowered to help the hurting as they *"go into all the world and make disciples of all nations, baptizing them in the name of the Father and of the Son and of the Holy Spirit"* -- Matthew 28:19. Baptizing as in dying and rising *with Christ. "And teaching them to obey everything I* (Jesus Christ, the Son) *have commanded you. And remember, I am with you* (there's that "with" word again) *to the end of the age"* -- Matthew 28:19.

That's what I mean by loving influence. The opposite of fearful control. The baptized Church will remember how this works. Our fearful control dies with that of Christ, so our loving influence can then rise with Christ. Our hurting can be what empowers our helping. Anything less is but a partial baptism or half a memory.

If Mark and Beth Wenzel can turn around the fear story that came with the traumatic death of their baby Alex, becoming the love story that is now going into all the world and making disciples, then there is hope for Christ's entire catholic Church. We really can have our next Great Awakening and again shepherd our nation in doing the same.

In some sense we are all prodigals getting ready for such a turn-around. Fear has driven us all to a point where something has to change. And it can change. Fear's heaviest stone can be rolled away, yet only when we awaken to the power our own loving action has to influence others. Such a re-awakening brings with it a new faith in love's resurrection. For ourselves. For our faith communities. And for the world God continues to so love.

About the Author

Daniel K. Held is both an Ohio Licensed Independent Social Worker and ordained United Methodist Elder (pastor) living with his wife of 51 years, Sue, in retirement. With degrees from Sterling College, the Ohio State University, and United Theological Seminary, he works intentionally to both improve and express his deeper understanding of God and people. Such understanding forms the basis for his faith and love of God, neighbor and self. His work included individual, marital and family counseling, educational workshops and seminars, pulpit ministry and writing over the span of now 50 years. The latter includes his blogsite: www.pastordanheldblog.com.

Other titles from Higher Ground Books & Media:

Wise Up to Rise Up by Rebecca Benston

A Path to Shalom by Steen Burke

From a Hole in My Life to a Life Made Whole by Janet Kay Teresa

Overcomer by Forrest Henslee

Miracles: I Love Them by Forest Godin

32 Days with Christ's Passion by Mark Etter

The Magic Egg by Linda Phillipson

The Tin Can Gang by Chuck David

Whobert the Owl by Mya C. Benston

For His Eyes Only by John Salmon

Out of Darkness by Stephen Bowman

Knowing Affliction and Doing Recovery by John Baldasare

Add these titles to your collection today!

http://highergroundbooksandmedia.com

Made in the USA
Lexington, KY
25 May 2019